HAYNES GUIDE
YELLOWSTONE NATIONAL PARK

REPLICA OF DIAMOND ANNIVERSARY MEDAL
(MEDALS ARE HAYNES' PRODUCT)

OLD FAITHFUL GEYSER AT UPPER GEYSER BASIN

HAYNES GUIDE

Handbook of
YELLOWSTONE NATIONAL PARK
By JACK ELLIS HAYNES

Approved by the
NATIONAL PARK SERVICE
DEPARTMENT OF THE INTERIOR

FORTY-NINTH REVISED EDITION
Illustrated
1947

Published by
HAYNES INC.

Yellowstone Park, Wyoming   Bozeman, Montana

UNITED STATES

DEPARTMENT OF THE INTERIOR

NATIONAL PARK SERVICE

CHICAGO 54, ILLINOIS

BASIC PHILOSOPHY OF THE NATIONAL PARK SERVICE

National parks are great places of America. Containing altogether 168 areas, the National Park System represents the effort of the Federal government to preserve, for the enjoyment of the people of the United States, the finest examples of the scenery of their country and the places of greatest significance from the standpoint of natural science, history and archeology. Twenty-seven areas are designated as "National Parks". There are also National Monuments, National Historic Sites, and other related types. Yellowstone National Park, first established of all this group, was "dedicated and set apart as a public park and pleasuring ground for the benefit and enjoyment of the people," and the act of establishment provided for the "preservation, from injury or spoilation, of all timber, mineral deposits, natural curiosities, or wonders within said park and their retention in their natural condition." As other areas were added to the System, and additional legislation regarding the parks found its way on to the statute books, the policy of preservation of all natural features was confirmed and strengthened. Thus a new concept of public land management was established.

When the National Park Service was established in 1916, the Congress defined the purposes of the reservations entrusted to its care in these words:

"to conserve the scenery and the natural and historic objects and the wildlife therein and to provide for the enjoyment of the same in such manner and by such means as will leave them unimpaired for the enjoyment of future generations."

In accordance with these mandates of Congress, the National parks are so managed that the public may enjoy them with the minimum of human interference with the natural processes—of forest and plant growth, of wildlife association, of geology. Wildlife is displayed under natural conditions. The miner seeks elsewhere the wealth that lies under the earth. Forests are protected for their beauty and interest and not as a source of lumber. Millions of visitors each year use, but do not consume, the natural resources of the parks. Though enjoyment by the public requires the construction of roads, campgrounds, and structures and utilities of various kinds, the ideal is to keep these intrusions to a minimum and to design them so as to harmonize with the landscape. All but a small fraction of the total area of the Yellowstone and other national parks remains as it was before the white man appeared on the American scene. Only in the parks is there assurance that Americans of the future will be able to see and enjoy some vestige of primitive wilderness as it was first revealed to the explorers and pioneers.

NEWTON B. DRURY
Director.

December 23, 1946.

UNITED STATES
DEPARTMENT OF THE INTERIOR
NATIONAL PARK SERVICE
YELLOWSTONE NATIONAL PARK
YELLOWSTONE PARK, WYO.

FOREWORD

The Haynes Guide to Yellowstone National Park is an authoritative compendium of information gleaned in the park in the course of more than sixty-five years by Frank Jay Haynes, one of the early pioneers of the region, and his son, Jack Ellis Haynes. The latter, who has spent every summer in Yellowstone since 1888, completely revised the Guide in 1942, and has brought the postwar edition up-to-date.

This little book will not only be of use to the visitor while in the park, pointing out to him points of interest that he might otherwise miss and generally giving him a helping hand; but it also will guide him through the pages of park history with the early explorers, soldiers, topographers, and other venturesome souls.

The 1947 edition of the Guide marks the 75th Anniversary of the establishment of the park in 1872 by act of Congress.

EDMUND B. ROGERS,
Superintendent.

June 1, 1947.

LOWER FALLS OF THE YELLOWSTONE RIVER
COPYRIGHT HAYNES INC.

PREFACE

We of today would have less foundation upon which to build a guidebook of Yellowstone National Park, were it not for the many stories about the Indians, fur traders, prospectors and explorers who frequented the region before its establishment as a national park, March 1, 1872; and the published works of those who participated in the official surveys and investigations conducted by the United States Government, begun in 1871. The region has irresistible attraction for scientists, educators and writers. It is not surprising, therefore, that publications concerning the park are numbered in tens of thousands.

Compiling a guidebook is something like a gold panning job involving the handling of many scoops of gravel for each nugget; and some prospecting too, so that recent natural changes and developments made by man, will not be overlooked.

General information about the park appears on pages 12 to 33, and in the historical chronology, pages 151 to 170.

The tour of the park, pages 34 to 149, which treats all of the important points of interest in the same sequence as they are encountered by visitors, includes distances, elevations, plant and animal life, geology, history, accommodations, services, illustrations and detail maps. Descriptions and road mileages begin at each park gate and at each of the principal road junctions. The story may be followed by those who tour any part of the park in the opposite direction, by reading the paragraphs in reverse order, and using the second, instead of the first mileage figures.

Specific information about any item or subject in this book, may be found by reference to the complete index. Symbols such as G2, show locations on the large map of the park, attached to the inside back cover.

No one can say how many authorities have been consulted in the accumulation of material for this text. Acknowledgments appear in several previous editions.

For most valuable assistance in revising this edition, we are especially indebted to:

—Edmund B. Rogers, Superintendent of Yellowstone National Park, whose counsel backed by intimate knowledge of the entire region and an appreciation of the viewpoints of park visitors, has been most helpful,

—Joseph Joffe, Assistant to the Superintendent, who offered many valuable suggestions, and capably reviewed the entire text for completeness and accuracy,

—Clyde Max Bauer, Ph.D., former Chief Park Naturalist, whose help in reviewing and expanding the geological and other scientific data, and checking the accuracy of the place names has been considerable, and

—David deL. Condon, Chief Park Naturalist of the Yellowstone. And to,

—George Marler, Ranger Naturalist, who suggested a number of changes in the tables of geysers which show height, duration and interval of each, and in descriptions of several geysers and hot springs.

Changes occurring in the park after this edition is printed, and before the next one is available, will be recorded on a Revision Sheet in the front part of this book, if deemed of sufficient importance.

Jack Ellis Haynes.

Yellowstone Park, Wyoming
June 1, 1947.

CONTENTS

GENERAL INFORMATION

TOUR OF THE PARK

TOUR OF THE PARK (Cont.)

HISTORICAL DATA

(Map of Yellowstone National Park; see inside back cover.)

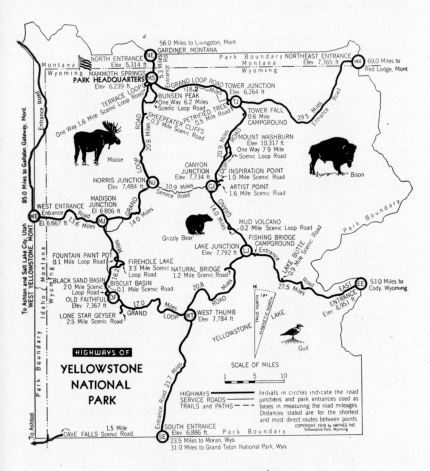

HIGHWAYS OF
**YELLOWSTONE
NATIONAL
PARK**

HIGHWAY SYSTEM

of

YELLOWSTONE NATIONAL PARK

(NOTE: Throughout this book are several detail maps of various **parts**
of the park; and a large, folded map of the entire park, attached **to the**
inside back cover).

YELLOWSTONE NATIONAL PARK MILEAGE TABLE

	Canyon Jct.	East Gate	Lake Jct.	Madison Jct.	Mammoth	Norris Jct.	North Gate	Northeast Gate	Old Faithful	South Gate	Tower Fall	Tower Jct.	West Gate	West Thumb
Canyon Jct...	.....	41.5	14.0	24.9	39.1[2]	10.9	44.4[2]	50.4	51.8[3]	56.5[3]	18.4	20.9	38.5	34.8
East Gate.....	41.5	....	27.5	81.5[3]	80.6[2]	52.4	85.9[2]	91.9	65.3[3]	70.0	59.9	62.4	95.1[3]	48.3
Lake Jct.,....	14.0	27.5	....	54.0[3]	53.1[2]	24.9	58.4[2]	64.4	37.8[3]	42.5	32.4	34.9	67.6[3]	20.8
Madison Jct...	24.9	81.5[3]	54.0[3]	....	34.8	14.0	40.1	75.3	16.2	54.9	43.3	45.8	13.6	33.2
Mammoth....	39.1[2]	80.6[2]	53.1[2]	34.8	....	20.8	5.3	47.7	51.0	89.7[1]	20.7	18.2	48.4	68.0[1]
Norris Jct.....	10.9	52.4	24.9	14.0	20.8	....	26.1	61.3	30.2	68.9[1]	29.3	31.8	27.6	47.2[1]
North Gate...	44.4[2]	85.9[2]	58.4[2]	40.1	5.3	26.1	....	53.0	56.3	95.0[1]	26.0	23.5	53.7	73.3[1]
Northeast Gate	50.4	91.9	64.4	75.3	47.7	61.3	53.0	......	91.5	106.9[2]	32.0	29.5	88.9	85.2
Old Faithful...	51.8[3]	65.3[3]	37.8[3]	16.2	51.0	30.2	56.3	91.5	....	38.7	59.5	62.0	29.8	17.0
South Gate...	56.5[3]	70.0	42.5	54.9	89.7[1]	68.9[1]	95.0[1]	106.9[2]	38.7	......	74.9	77.4	68.5	21.7
Tower Fall....	18.4	59.9	32.4	43.3	20.7	29.3	26.0	32.0	59.5	74.9	....	2.5	56.9	53.2
Tower Jct.....	20.9	62.4	34.9	45.8	18.2	31.8	23.5	29.5	62.0	77.4	2.5	....	59.4	55.7
West Gate....	38.5	95.1[3]	67.6[3]	13.6	48.4	27.6	53.7	88.9	29.8	68.5	56.9	59.4	....	46.8
West Thumb..	34.8	48.3	20.8	33.2	68.0[1]	47.2[1]	73.3[1]	85.2[2]	17.0	21.7	53.2	55.7	46.8	....

1—Via Old Faithful.   2—Via Tower Fall.   3—Via West Thumb.

The highway system of Yellowstone National Park has about 300 miles of which 97.6 are entrance roads, 141.9 The Grand Loop Road of the Park, and about 60.5 miles are side roads, most of which are short, scenic loop roads, or spurs.

Entrance roads begin at the park gates and connect with The Grand Loop Road of the Park. Locations and distances traversed by these entrance roads in the park are: North, 5.3 miles; West, 13.6 miles; South, 21.7 miles; East, 27.5 miles; and Northeast, 29.5 miles.

Park tours, regardless of the gates used, as entrances and exits, can be arranged to include all of The Grand Loop Road of the Park. The distances traversed by those who enter the park and leave it by the same gate, are: North, 152.5 miles; West, 169.1 miles; South, 185.3 miles; East, 196.9 miles; and Northeast, 200.9 miles.

The Grand Loop Road of the Park, outstanding, scenic highway of the region—141.9 miles in all—connects Mammoth Hot Springs, (park headquarters), with the geyser basins, Yellowstone Lake, Grand Canyon of the Yellowstone, and Tower Fall.

Acknowledged to be one of the most magnificent scenic tours in America, it should be traveled leisurely, and completely.

MADONNA OF THE WILDS

GENERAL INFORMATION

Yellowstone National Park, established on March 1, 1872, by an Act of Congress of the United States of America, is mostly in northwestern Wyoming, but extends also into the states of Montana and Idaho.

It was set apart not only to preserve its geysers which number more than two hundred, its terraces, and other thermal features, but to protect the entire area and its wildlife in order that people from all lands may benefit by seeing and enjoying its countless attractions. In its 3,471.51 square miles are large numbers of wild animals including bison, moose, wapiti, deer, pronghorns, bighorns, and both grizzly and black bears, all living in their native environment.

Elevations in the park range from about 5,000 feet near the Yellowstone River at the north to 11,360 feet, the summit of Eagle Peak near the southeast corner. The park roads range in elevation from 5,314 feet at the North Entrance to 10,317 feet on the summit of Mount Washburn, reached by the Chittenden Road, a side loop route, which ascends the mountain on its southwest slope from Dunraven Pass and descends the north slope, rejoining The Grand Loop Road 5 miles further on toward Tower Fall.

Although precise elevations of all the bench marks have been determined to within 1/1000 of a foot, those appearing on the maps and in the text of this handbook are in all cases the nearest even foot.

Climate. The park is ideal as a summer retreat from hotter sections of the country. Rainstorms, usually of short duration, are common but the atmosphere is comparatively dry. Even during the hottest portion of the summer, evenings and nights are always cool. The highest temperature ever recorded at Mammoth was 92.4° (Aug. 12, 1940). The lowest temperature ever recorded in the continental United States on an official Weather Bureau thermometer, 66° below zero, (Feb. 9, 1933), was recorded at Riverside Station in Yellowstone National Park, near the West Gate. The highest and lowest temperatures ever recorded at Mammoth were 92.4° (Aug. 12, 1940), and 39.6° below zero (Feb. 9, 1933). Maximum snow (undrifted) depths recorded in 1936 in these areas: (February 25) West Entrance 60 inches; (March 29) Bechler Ranger Station 89 inches, South Entrance 85 inches, Old Faithful 72 inches; (April 3) Tower Fall 28 inches. The average annual snowfall at Mammoth is 91 inches; at higher elevations in the park it is more.

Up to the present time less than five hundred of the many thousand **thermal features** in the park have been named. Of hot springs alone, Dr. A. C.

Peale estimated there are three thousand, while Dr. Arnold Hague, also of the United States Geological Survey, said the number "probably exceeds twenty-five hundred." Few visitors realize the vast extent of these hot areas, and the almost countless number of thermal features, due probably to the fact that many geyser basins and other thermal areas are not reached by the highways. There are at least ten thousand separate and distinct thermal features of all kinds in the park. The Grand Loop Road of the Park and the system of footpaths make accessible some of the finest examples, yet numerous others, also of first magnitude, lie in the wilderness areas and are, therefore, seldom visited.

Yellowstone scenery is enthralling. Mountains, canyons, streams, waterfalls, lakes, and forests present ever-changing panoramas as visitors travel over the approach and entrance roads and The Grand Loop Road of the Park, which Grand Loop connects the principal geyser basins, Yellowstone Lake, the Grand Canyon of the Yellowstone, Mount Washburn, Tower Fall and Mammoth Hot Springs.

Here is a Mecca for geologists and other students of nature, for sight-seers, camerists, fishermen, and recreationists.

One of the most important historical documents in the development of the present national park system, is quoted:

The Act of Dedication of Yellowstone National Park.

Approved March 1, 1872

BE IT ENACTED BY THE SENATE AND THE HOUSE OF REPRESENTATIVES OF THE UNITED STATES OF AMERICA IN CONGRESS ASSEMBLED,

That the tract of land in the Territories of Montana and Wyoming, lying near the headwaters of the Yellowstone River, and described as follows, to-wit: Commencing at the junction of Gardiner's River with the Yellowstone River, and running east to the meridian passing ten miles to the eastward of the most eastern point of Yellowstone Lake; thence south along the said meridian to the parallel of latitude passing ten miles south of the most southern point of Yellowstone Lake; thence west along said parallel to the meridian passing fifteen miles west of the most western point of Madison Lake; thence north along said meridian to the latitude of the junction of the Yellowstone and Gardiner's Rivers; thence east to the place of beginning—is hereby reserved and withdrawn from settlement, occupancy or sale under the laws of the United States, and dedicated and set apart as a public park or pleasuring ground for the benefit and enjoyment of the people; and all persons who shall locate, or settle upon or occupy the same or any part thereof, except as hereinafter provided, shall be considered trespassers and removed therefrom.

Sec. 2. That said public Park shall be under the exclusive control of the Secretary of the Interior, whose duty it shall be, as soon as practicable, to make and publish such rules and regulations as he may deem necessary or proper for the care and management of the same. Such regulations shall provide for the preservation from injury or spoliation of all timber, mineral deposits, natural curiosities or wonders within said park and their retention in their natural condition.

The Secretary may, in his discretion, grant leases for building purposes, for terms not exceeding ten years, of small parcels of ground, at such places in said park as shall require the erection of buildings for the accommodation of visitors; all of the proceeds of said leases, and all other revenues that may be derived from any source connected with said park, to be expended under his direction, in the management of the same, and the construction of roads and bridle paths therein. He shall provide against the wanton destruction of the fish and game found within said park, and against their capture or destruction for the purposes of merchandise or profit. He shall also cause all persons trespassing upon the same after the passage of this act to be removed therefrom and generally shall be authorized to take all such measures as shall be necessary or proper to fully carry out the objects and purposes of this act."

It is significant that the present status of Yellowstone National Park antedated the formal admission to statehood of the three surrounding states by almost two decades. Montana Territory was created in 1864 and was admitted to statehood in 1889; the Territory of Idaho was organized in 1863 and was admitted to the Union as a state in 1890; Wyoming was established as a territory by Act of Congress in 1868 and was formally admitted as a state in 1890.

The park, roughly rectangular in shape, has had its boundaries modified only twice. The east boundary and the northwest corner were changed in 1929, to include the Hoodoo region at the east, and the petrifactions at the northwest, and to conform more closely to the drainage divides; in 1932 a win-

EDMUND B. ROGERS
SUPERINTENDENT OF YELLOWSTONE
NATIONAL PARK—APPOINTED
MAY 25, 1936

ter wild animal grazing area, near the North Entrance, was added to the park.

Administration of the park vested in the National Park Service of the Department of the Interior, is directed by the superintendent, with headquarters at Mammoth.

The protection division. Uniformed rangers of the protection division man the checking stations at all park entrances and ranger stations in other important areas throughout the park. Operations during the travel season are handled by the permanent staff augmented by a force of temporary rangers. The entire area is patrolled by rangers to protect this vast property and its native wildlife as well as the hundreds of thousands of visitors each season, who come from all countries. On several mountaintops a r e lightning-proof fire lookouts, manned day and night in summer by lookouts who spot forest fires. Rangers, who patrol the roads, operate cars equipped with radios for communication with the headquarters short-wave station at Mammoth. Forest fire patrols use portable two-way radio sets. All checking stations at entrances, ranger stations, fire lookouts, and patrols at intervals along the roads, have telephone service day and night. The protection division handles forest insect control, provides both forest and building fire protection, maintains trails, protects wildlife, takes a wild animal census annually, supervises fish planting, and handles law enforcement.

The naturalist division operates museums and information offices, manned by ranger naturalists, at Mammoth, Norris, Madison Junction, Upper Geyser Basin, and Fishing Bridge Campground. This division maintains several field exhibits along the roads for the information of visitors. The permanent staff is augmented during the summer by a corps of ranger naturalists especially fitted for their work. They conduct parties over the formations at Mammoth and the geyser basins at Norris, Old Faithful, and West Thumb, and other sightseeing trips afoot. They guide automobile sightseeing caravans and wild animal stalks, lecture in the amphitheaters at the principal concentration points of visitors, and c o n d u c t campfire programs. This division, under the direction of the chief park naturalist, also maintains a library at Mammoth, conducts historical and scientific research and issues publications.

The engineering division directs road and maintenance work and has charge of all general engineering projects in the park, including surveys, preparations of maps and plans for water and sewer installations, topographic surveys, d e s i g n and construction of government buildings, and other physical improvements.

The sanitation d i v i s i o n handles maintenance, operation, and construction work on water and sewer systems, rest rooms, incinerators, and heating plants.

The communications a n d electrical division supervises the power plants, all electrical installations, the short-wave radios, and the telephone system.

The mechanical and s h o p division maintains all trucks,

tractors, graders, p u m p i n g plants, fire fighting equipment and other equipment.

Government agencies which cooperate with the National Park Service include the Public Roads Administration, Public Health Service, Bureau of Entomology, Fish and Wildlife Service, Forest Service, Geological Survey, War Department, Weather Bureau, Post Office Department and Department of Justice.

The **Public Roads Administration** of the Federal Works Agency, since 1926 has engineered the construction and improvement of the major Yellowstone Park highway system under an inter-bureau agreement with the National Park Service. Since 1931 this work has also included park approach roads. Quoting B. W. Matteson, district engineer:

"The highway improvements made since 1926 have followed in general the original location of the approximately 300 mile system, which so admirably serves entrance and exit travel to and from the park, as well as between the various attractive features within the park. Where considerable advantage could be derived, such as shortening distance between major points of interest and through comparatively unattractive terrain, or reducing the necessary rise and fall, some relocations have been made, but only where esthetic features, as well as good engineering practice, could be equally well provided for. Highway improvement in the park can only be carried on during the period from about May 15 to October 15 each year and during that time a field office of the bureau is maintained in one of the government administrative buildings at Mammoth."

The **Fish and Wildlife Service** at Yellowstone Lake station handles large numbers of trout eggs. As high as forty million eggs have been collected in one year. The rainbow trout eggs are collected at Trout Lake and M o n t a n a grayling e g g s a t Grebe Lake. Cutthroat, Montana grayling, rainbow, Loch Leven, and eastern b r o o k (speckled) trout are planted in the various streams and lakes of the park, so that none of these waters will become depleted of game fish.

The **Weather Bureau** at Mammoth operated the year around ever since the building was erected in 1903, was abandoned in 1941. Observations were recorded in the park ever since the bureau was started by the U. S. Army in 1872. In 1892 it was transferred to the Dept. of Agriculture, and in 1940 to the Dept. of Commerce.

W e a t h e r observations are now made by park rangers and furnished the U. S. Weather Bureau.

The **Department of Justice is** represented in the park by the Hon. T. Paul Wilcox, U. S. Commissioner. He was appointed July 1, 1935, by Hon. T. Blake Kennedy, U. S. District Judge for the District of Wyoming, upon the retirement of Hon. John W. Meldrum, first U. S. Commissioner i n t h e park, who had served continuously since 1894. The Chief

Ranger and four of his assistants are Deputy U. S. Marshals, regularly commissioned as such by the the U. S. Marshal for the District of Wyoming.

The U. S. Commissioner has original jurisdiction over misdemeanors committed in the park, and has authority to summarily hear and dispose of such cases, and assess penalties to a maximum of $500, six months in jail or both. In case of a felony—a crime carrying a penalty of imprisonment in a penitentiary — t h e Commissioner acts as a committing magistrate comparable to a Justice of the Peace, admitting defendants to bond and fixing the amount, for their appearance before the U. S. District Court at Cheyenne, Wyoming.

"The principal misdemeanors" to quote Commissioner Wilcox "are violations of the Rules and Regulations promulgated by the Secretary of the Interior for the safety and comfort of park visitors, and for the protection of wild life and the natural features of the park. The more frequent violations are: defacing in any manner, formations, buildings, etc., destroying the beauty of hot springs, pools and geysers by throwing objects into them, building fires outside of the regularly designated camp sites, taking too many fish, and driving recklessly or in excess of the prescribed speed limits. It is apparent that most of the infractions are acts of thoughtlessness on the part of visitors which seem insignificant in the individual case, but when multiplied by thousands the resultant damage is incalculable."

Church services scheduled for each year on Sundays from June to September include Protestant, Roman Catholic, and Latter Day Saints (Mormon) services in the chapel at Mammoth. Sunday services are also scheduled at the lodges at Old Faithful, Lake, and Canyon. (See posted schedules.)

Mountain standard time, adopted in the United States by the railroads since 1883 and approved by Congress (1918) applies to the entire park. It is one hour later than Pacific, one hour earlier than Central, and two hours earlier than Eastern Standard Time.

United States mail for rail passengers and motorists patronizing hotels and lodges should be addressed in care of some specific hotel or lodge in "Yellowstone Park, Wyoming;" otherwise it should be addressed to "General Delivery, Yellowstone Park, Wyoming." All general delivery mail should be called for at the post office at Mammoth.

No mail should be addressed in care of a "park entrance."

Outgoing first-class mail may be left at Haynes picture shops, in hotels, lodges, and campgrounds, at which places also postage stamps are sold for the convenience of patrons. This service is supplementary to the general postal service available at the United States post office at Mammoth (open the year-round) and the postal stations at Old Faithful, West Thumb, Lake, Fishing Bridge Campground, and at the Canyon —all of which have daily "star route" service to and from Mammoth during the summer season.

The postmaster suggests that on outgoing mail the address be complete and that sufficient postage be affixed, because in past seasons much undeliverable mail has accumulated.

Public telephone service to any place in the world where service is available can be furnished from the principal centers in the park—Mammoth, Old Faithful, Lake, Fishing Bridge, Canyon, and Camp Roosevelt—during the park season.

This service, installed in the park in 1927, and owned by the American Telephone and Telegraph Company, is operated by the Mountain States Telephone and Telegraph Company.

There are about 200 miles of copper circuits in the park. Standard equipment throughout has made possible the very finest service.

Public telephone service is not available at museums or ranger stations except in cases where charges can be made collect, or charges reversed, as rangers and employees of the government are not permitted to collect moneys for services rendered over the lines, except in extreme emergencies.

One of the emergencies which not infrequently occurs, is an emergency due to a bear bite or dangerous scratch inflicted upon an unsuspecting tourist who has ignored the prominent, but often disregarded warning NOT to feed the bears! (Those of us who live in the park are AFRAID of bears.)

Prior to the advent (1915) of automobiles in the park the length of the tourist season was determined largely by the operation of the hotels and lodges, daily railway service, and stage-coach service, which was about three months each year. Since then the constantly increasing flow of automobile travel has created a demand both for more accommodations and for a longer period, resulting in large developments in all campgrounds and related facilities, including cafeterias, cabins, camp sites, general stores, filling stations, and picture shops, which now serve the public for 5 to 6 months each year, augmenting the regular hotel, lodge, furnished cabin, and bus service, which is still maintained for about 3 months. The condition of the park roads is now the only factor that determines the length of the tourist season, which begins in early May, as soon as the snowplows have broken through, and continues usually until late October. Campgrounds and related facilities are put in operation each season as soon as the volume of travel warrants, and not all continue in operation until late October, but enough facilities are available for motorists to give adequate service from May 1 to Oct. 15. The road from Gardiner via Mammoth, Tower

Junction and Northeast Gate to Cooke, Montana, is kept open the year-round.

The best time to visit the park? That is not easy to say. The day by day travelgraph looks like the sky line of a high mountain, beginning from and ending on a zero base line and having two tremendous mid-season peaks—one in late July, and a still higher one between August 5 and 10, the period of greatest travel being from mid-July to mid-August.

All of the facilities of the concessioners and the government are in full operation each year from mid-June until September. During the month of May, the first half of June, the last half of September, and all of October, accommodations, while ample to take care of the requirements of visitors, are curtailed to a degree commensurate with the demand; some units are not then in operation.

Camerists have several facts to consider. It is impossible to get full illumination on the Grand Canyon late in the season as the sun is too far south, yet the gorgeous autumnal colorings especially in the groves of aspens, which take on brilliant gold and Indian-red colors, as well as the fiery color of some bushes and undergrowth in the forest, and exceptional opportunities to photograph the large grazing and browsing animals seeking the lower elevations near the roads at that time, are compensatory. In the late fall (if dry) the atmosphere may not be clear due to pollen and dust in the air, and smoke from forest fires which may be a hundred or more miles distant, as well as streaky cirrus clouds of minute ice crystals in the sky. In early spring the waterfalls are, of course, much more luxuriant than in late fall. In the spring the air is clear, making distant shots usually possible; and the vegetation is greener and flowers more abundant. The flowering plants, however, begin to bloom while the snow is still on the ground in the spring, and although many have seeded and vanished by fall, others will then be found in full bloom—the pageantry of flowers making a continuous, ever-changing parade throughout the season. Midseason is best for photographing hot pools, which at other times are likely to be more heavily veiled in steam. Geysers are best photographed in spring or fall when the cooler atmosphere is conducive to larger clouds of billowing steam, and in early morning and late afternoon, on comparatively still days. The large, flocculent cumulus clouds, which adorn so many prize pictures, may be photographed at intervals throughout the entire season but since they are at their best for only a few hours at a time one should not delay photographing them, as in the mountainous country they do not remain stationary long.

In early spring the animals migrate to higher elevations; this is the season when the young are born and are zealously guarded by the mothers.

Animals change so much during the cycle of seasons each year that they should be photographed in each stage; and the young change so rapidly that an interesting series of progress pictures can be made in a few months.

The fishing season in the park is usually from sunrise May 30 to sunset October 15. Some waters afford their best fishing early in the summer when the waters have cleared from the spring freshets while others are sought in the early fall. The month of July is regarded as the best of the season for fishing, with August probably the poorest.

Those who desire to visit the park when comparatively few people are there will find the roads, parking areas, campgrounds, and other facilities much less crowded if they avoid the period of greatest travel (July 15-August 15).

The conclusion must necessarily be—come when you can —in the winter on the days set for skiing and photographing the remarkable wildlife—or in the spring—or anytime before the fall snows block the roads. Each act in the great drama of Yellowstone has some high spot different from, and not eclipsed by the others.

Motorists are cautioned to drive with exceptional care within the park as in such an area, devoted as it is to sightseeing and recreation, many persons are prone to drive on the wrong side of the road, to park at extremely dangerous places, and do many things which jeopardize themselves and others, while they are entranced with the scenic beauty of the park, its wildlife, or its natural wonders.

Air Lines serve the park during the summers from all parts of the country. Airports are near the park at West Yellowstone and other centers. Within the park itself there are no airports nor landing fields.

Bus Lines. Transcontinental bus lines serve Cody, Wyoming, and Livingston, Bozeman and West Yellowstone, Montana. Connection is made with the park buses at Gardiner, Montana (reached by bus or train from Livingston), and at Bozeman, West Yellowstone and Cody.

Radio reception, due to a combination of distance, mountainous terrain and varying atmospheric conditions in the park, is consistently poor in the daytime. Broadcasts are heard much better after nightfall when reception is frequently excellent.

Railways serving Yellowstone Park are the Northern Pacific Railway, the Union Pacific Railroad, The Milwaukee Road, and the Burlington Route.

The Northern Pacific Railway operates to and from Gardiner, Montana, passengers using the North Entrance of the park; to and from Red Lodge, Montana, passengers using connecting buses between that point and Northeast Entrance, and to and from Bozeman, Montana, passengers using connecting buses between that point and the West Entrance; the Union Pacific Railroad operates to and from West Yellowstone, Montana, passengers using the West Entrance, and to and from Victor, Idaho, passengers using the South Entrance; The Milwaukee Road operates to and from Gallatin Gateway, Montana, passengers using Yellowstone Park Company buses between there and the West Entrance; and the Burlington Route operates to and from Cody, Wyoming, passengers using Yellowstone Park Company buses between Cody and the East Entrance.

Concessioners, all of which conduct their enterprises in the park under franchises from the Government, o c c u p y lands leased from the Government; but the buildings and equipment they use in the park are owned by the concessioners. The Government regulates the types of service performed and the prices charged.

The names of concessioners and data concerning each, follow:

The Yellowstone Park Company. The transportation division of this company operates the yellow buses within the park to and from all entrances, connecting with the railroads at the north and west boundaries and at the nearest points outside of the park served by other railroad and bus lines. In

the park, in conjunction with general store concessions, they operate the service stations at all points except at Tower Fall. At Camp Roosevelt gas and oil are available in emergencies.

Their public garages are at Gardiner, Mammoth, U p p e r Geyser Basin, Lake, and Canyon. Repair shops are operated in connection with the garages, and there is one also in the Fishing Bridge Campground.

The hotel department of the company operates Mammoth Springs Hotel, with a group of guest cottages, dining room and the Terrace Grill; Old Faithful Inn at Upper Geyser Basin and Lake and Canyon hotels. All of these supply the highest type of service, comparable in facilities and accommodations, to the best city hotels. In most of the hotels are picture shops operated by Haynes Inc., as well as newsstands, curio shops and cocktail lounges.

The lodge division of the company operates the lodges at Upper Geyser Basin, Lake, and Canyon. At all of the lodges are furnished guest cabins, large dining rooms, recreation halls and other facilities f o r the accommodation of guests. In most of the lodges are picture shops operated by Haynes Inc. and curio shops, operated by Hamilton Stores, Inc. Cafeterias are operated in connection with the group of tourist cabins in the campgrounds at Upper Geyser Basin, West Thumb, Fishing Bridge, and Canyon. Camp Roosevelt, near Tower Junction, has a large main building with a dining room and groups of furnished and unfurnished cabins. It also operates a group of tourist cabins in the campground at Mammoth. Woodyards, supplying sawed and split wood, are located near the principal campgrounds.

The boat division of the company operates a fleet of sightseeing boats on Yellowstone Lake and a large number of small boats for fishing at West Thumb, Lake and Fishing Bridge, having boathouses and docks at these points. A favorite fishing excursion is from the Lake boathouse to Stevenson Island.

Saddle horses are available at Mammoth Springs Hotel, at both the inn and the lodge at Upper Geyser Basin, and at both the hotel and lodge at Canyon, for both fishing and sight-seeing trips, with guides.

Hamilton Stores, Inc., operates general stores and filling stations at Upper Geyser Basin, West Thumb, Lake, and Fishing Bridge and the curio shops in the lodges at Old Faithful Lake, and Canyon.

Charles Ashworth Hamilton, president of the company, acquired the Klamer general store at Upper Geyser Basin in 1915. In 1916 he opened the filling stations at both Upper Geyser Basin and West Thumb and the general stores at West Thumb and Lake. In 1917 he opened the general store in the campground at Upper Geyser Basin, the filling station at Lake, and Fishing Bridge general store and filling station. In 1930 he opened the filling station in the campground at Upper Geyser Basin. In 1931 he took over operation of the curio shops in the lodges at Mammoth, Old Faithful, Lake, and Canyon. Hamilton's connection with the park dates back to 1905, when he was first employed by the Yellowstone Park Association.

Pryor Stores. Anna K. Pryor and Elizabeth Trischman acquired the establishment of Ole Anderson at Mammoth in 1908, and organized the Park Curio Shop and Coffee Shop there. They later purchased the general stores and filling stations near Mammoth Springs Hotel and near Canyon Junction, and the grocery in the Mammoth Campground from George Whittaker. Included in their operations are the cafeteria and curio shop which they built in the Mammoth Campground.

Mrs. Pryor and Miss Trischman are the daughters of the late George Trischman, who died in 1929, and who was a pioneer in the park, being at one time in the military service and later a government contractor.

Haynes Inc. with headquarters at Mammoth, supplies a wide assortment of pictorial souvenirs, photographs, guidebooks and other publications, postcards, films, photographic supplies, lithographs, etchings,

HEADQUARTERS SHOP OF HAYNES INC., AT MAMMOUTH HOT SPRINGS

etc. Its **picture shops** throughout the park, are at Mammoth, Old Faithful, West Thumb, Fishing Bridge, Canyon and Tower Fall areas and in most of the hotels and lodges. At Tower Fall and Camp Roosevelt it does a **general store** business too, including refreshment and soda fountain service; and at Tower Fall supplies delicatessen and lunch service.

The history of this company dates back to 1881, when Frank Jay Haynes (1853-1921), its founder, first came to the park. Jack E. Haynes, his son, who has been in the park summers, ever since 1888, has managed the enterprise since 1916.

Winter address: Haynes Bldg., 801 N. Wallace Ave., Bozeman, Montana.

Medical service for park visitors and employees of the government and companies operating in the park, has headquarters at Mammoth. Trained nurses are stationed at hotels and lodges, which establishments have well-equipped dispensaries. Physicians of the medical staff have ambulance and transportation facilities, and will attend patients at any place in the park upon call. In emergency any park ranger or employee of any company operating in the park will assist in securing the nearest available medical service quickly. A physician or nurse may be summoned by telephone at any hotel, lodge, ranger station, store or picture shop. A staff of three physicians and eighteen or more nurses comprises the personnel of the hospital at Mammoth and the service in hotels and lodges during the summer season, and the year around institution in Livingston, Montana.

Dr. George A. Windsor under whose direction the medical service in the park has been conducted since 1924, (1947) in partnership with doctors A. M. Lueck and John A. Pearson, comments on feeding bears:

"Our experience shows some lessening in bear bites as a result of repeated warnings against feeding bears by hand. It is difficult to get the public to appreciate the folly of such a pastime that might at any time become dangerous, as long as some people seem to enjoy the thrill of being bitten by a bear."

As to overexertion in high altitudes he says:

"It is suggested that older people, and those in otherwise weakened condition, should limit their activities while in the park, as high altitude and fatigue of travel put added strain on one's whole physical being—particularly on the heart and blood vessels."

The government has established public **campgrounds** at several important stopping places, where pure water, sanitation facilities, and some equipment are supplied for the free use of campers. The use of these campgrounds, with fire protection, sanitation, stores, shops, and other facilities, is encouraged rather than promiscuous camping in outlying areas.

On the theory that the park itself offers such a wide variety of natural attractions for the entertainment of the guests, it has never been considered necessary to provide such facilities as golf links, tennis courts, and motion picture theaters, common to many summer resorts, the principal outdoor sports in the park being sightseeing, photographing and fishing trips, either on horseback or on foot, and boat trips.

The **Howard Eaton Trail,** named for Howard Eaton, famous Western horseman and guide, was dedicated in 1923. In general it follows The Grand Loop Road of the Park, and leads to the many points of interest in the park. It is one of the most scenic trails in America for horseback riders covering a roundtrip distance of about 150 miles.

Wild animal trails. Anyone who leaves the beaten paths and travels the wilderness areas of the park will be impressed not only by the great number of wild animal trails, that antedate human civilization, but also by the skill displayed by the dumb animals, who made and keep up these trails, in selecting passes and routes for their use. The Grand Loop Road, the entrance roads, and ranger trails of today follow in general some of the routes used by the wild animals before this area was even known to man.

Even the wild animals will seek the open meadows for safety when high winds threaten to blow down trees—another example of woodcraft which humans have learned from dumb animals. From the Indians experienced campers have learned the practice of economy in the use of firewood, as a squaw can cook for her whole family for a week with the same amount of fuel that some white brothers use to toast a few marshmallows.

Fishing is one of the finest recreations in the park. The season: May 30 to October 15. The numerous lakes and streams are teeming with fighting trout and during most of the summer the angler can catch his limit of cutthroat, rainbow, Loch Leven or brook trout. Montana grayling and Mackinaw trout are found in some of the waters. Even inexperienced fishermen can catch native trout in Yellowstone Lake or in the Yellowstone River between Lake and Canyon, and especially at Fishing Bridge where thousands of trout are taken.

The month of July affords the best fishing of the season while good results may be had in some of the streams after the middle of August and until about the end of September. Artificial flies and spinners are the chief lures. Late May and early June are best for the bait fisherman. Rangers throughout the park are informed of the best fishing in their particular districts and will gladly impart fishing information to the inquiring visitor.

No fishing license is required in the park. The limit per day for each person fishing is 15 pounds of fish (dressed weight with heads and tails intact), plus 1 fish, not to exceed 10 fish, in most of the waters of the park; and 10 pounds, plus 1 fish, not to exceed 5 fish, in

certain posted waters. Fishing tackle can be purchased at all of the general stores in the park and can be rented from the porters at the hotels and lodges. Boats can be rented at several places on Yellowstone Lake and fishing tackle is also available. For those desiring the more strenuous fishing expeditions, trips can be made on horseback with experienced guides to some of the choicest fishing holes in the park.

Fred J. Foster, former asst. regional director of the Fish and Wildlife Service of the Department of Interior, says:

"Yellowstone Park has probably the finest trout fishing, where the waters are easily accessible, of any place in the United States, and even those visitors unfamiliar with trout fishing may catch trout in Yellowstone Lake by trolling, from June 20 to July 31.

"Yellowstone River, between Fishing Bridge and Canyon, is one of the finest 'dry fly' streams to be found anywhere, being particularly good in July and August in the late afternoon or evening, when dry flies of very small size are used. The Firehole and Madison rivers are excellent for both wet and dry fly fishing during the month of June and also in September and October. The Lamar and lower Yellowstone rivers in the park are best during late July, August and September, after the waters clear from the early summer flood conditions. Many of the smaller streams are excellent throughout the entire season.

"Excellent Mackinaw trout fishing may be found in Shoshone, Lewis and Heart lakes, the record weight Mackinaw being 37 pounds for Lewis Lake. Those lakes also contain other species such as the native, blackspotted, eastern brook, and/or Loch Leven trout."

A park regulation reads:

"Use or possession of salmon eggs, or other fish eggs, either fresh or preserved, or live or dead minnows, chubs, or other bait fish, digging of worms, and canning or curing of fish are prohibited."

Although little if any mention is made of **insects** in literature describing the park, there is a large variety of these wild inhabitants. Those which fishermen are most interested in avoiding are mosquitoes, deer flies, and horseflies, which fortunately do not bother them the whole season but principally in the spring. They are no more numerous in this region than in other similar areas but are mentioned to forewarn those who plan on spending considerable time out of doors in the park. The wapiti and mule deer, and some other wild animals, are hosts of the woodtick, which is bothersome only in the early part of each season.

Photographing in the Yellowstone has become the most universally popular of the several outstanding and associated pastimes in the park—photographing, horseback riding, and fishing. Taking pictures in natural colors, either stills or motion pictures, is rapidly supplanting monochrome photography. The beautiful colorings of the terraces, hot pools, and other thermal features of the park, and the gorgeous chasm of the Yellowstone, which so long defied even the great artists of the world who endeavored to reproduce it, are ideal subjects for the camerist of today, and the results obtained are strikingly realistic and beautiful.

Killing a wild animal or bird is not nearly so great a feat as photographing it. Few other places, if any, afford such admirable opportunities for photographing animals and birds in their natural haunts.

Wild flowers, too, of which there are over a thousand different species in the park, are ideal subjects.

Probably the most important consideration in obtaining successful photographs is keeping the equipment and instruments clean and in proper adjustment. To clean lenses, filters, and other optical glass used on cameras and projectors, flick off dust with lens tissue or a soft camel's hair brush, then breathe on the glass and wipe it gently with lens tissue. Lint from lens tissue is then brushed off. One should avoid touching the glass surfaces or allowing the skin to come in contact with them. No solvents should be used except those recommended by lens makers. Exposing lenses or filters to direct sunlight, excessive moisture or heat may injure them as materials used in cementing lenses and filters are affected by both heat and moisture. Optical glass is relatively soft and easily scratched. Lenses and filters which are scratched or not clean, or those in which the cement has deteriorated cannot produce perfect pictures. Spray from geysers, if allowed to dry on a lens or filter, may spot it. Raindrops or spray from waterfalls, also, should not be allowed to dry on the glass surfaces.

Stalking wild animals by automobile from the road is a sport enjoyed by a large percentage of the motorists in the park. Due to their protective colorations, which even change with the seasons of the year, it is easy to pass by wild animals and birds along the road without seeing them. The driver, whose attention is practically always either on the road or on highway traffic, seldom spots any wildlife, so the responsibility is up to the passengers. Cameras should always be kept cocked and loaded ready for use, as it is possible many times to take splendid pictures from the car after it has been brought to a stop. It is ofttimes possible to take better pictures from within rather than outside of the car as the approach of humans and the slamming of car doors frequently startles the wild animals, who are able to move away from the road with remarkable agility, and it is a habit of wild beasts to turn their backs in disdain upon people who intrude themselves into their presence.

Underexposure is a common fault of many pictures of animals. If a bear is black it is easy to make an underexposure; if animals are sheltered in the timber the light on them is less intense than it appears to the eye.

No one attempts to stalk animals even by automobile while making sounds that may disturb them. One reason Indians wear moccasins is to make paws of their feet, which tread the wilderness silently.

During the past few winter seasons special days have been set aside for **winter sports**, in connection with the photographing of wild animals in winter, a sport much more exciting and difficult than hunting them with guns. These gatherings have been held in the vicinity of Mammoth, Tower Fall, and the Buffalo Ranch, the only suitable sections of the park kept open for any winter travel, and they have proven very popular with the devotees of both ski and camera.

Yellowstone Park is in the heart of the **dude ranch country** of the three adjoining states. Many of the dude ranches include a park trip, as well as attendance at one or more of the rodeos nearby, in the entertainment of their guests, during the summer season. Many of the park visitors, likewise, avail themselves of the gracious hospitality of the dude ranchers, and spend parts of their vacations enjoying the comfortable facilities of these ranches and life in the "cow country". In the fall of the year the ranch hunting parties depend for their game, to a great extent, upon the great reservoir of **wildlife** bred within the sanctuary of the park. One of the results of the preservation of wildlife within the park, is that there is a supply of game for the many hunters, who come from all parts of the world to these neighboring hunting grounds. Inasmuch as the wild animals, while in the park, are protected from man, their worst enemy, it is reasonable to assume that at certain times there will be a surplus of some of the many different species, as has been the case in the past with the wapiti, and some of the other grazing and browsing animals.

The game and fish departments of the adjacent states do well to cooperate with the officials of the National Park Service in timing their **hunting seasons** (outside the park), so that the kill each year may be commensurate with the surplus game available. The Fish and Wildlife Service, operating the hatchery at Yellowstone Lake, in cooperation with the National Park Service, supplies game fish to Montana, Wyoming and Idaho, and other states, after the requirements of the park waters have been met, and all sportsmen who hunt and fish in this great area owe their appreciation to the park, at least in part, for the fine fishing and hunting that they enjoy.

Yellowstone lingo used by employees (more commonly by lodge employees) includes:
Dude, bus tourist, either sex.
Dudine, lady tourist.
Dude wrangler, h o r s e m a n-guide.
Savage, an employee, either sex.
Gear jammer, bus driver.
Song wrangler, hostess at lodge.
Pillow puncher, cabin girl.
Pearl diver, dishwasher.
Bubble queen, laundry worker.

Heaver, waitress.
Packrat, porter at lodge.
Rats' nest, porters' dormitory.
Ninety day wonder, temporary summer ranger.
Formation, or
Formation dance, dance open to the public and employees.
Rotten logging, spooning.

Lingo characteristic especially of the pre-automobile era when stagecoach drivers and soldiers were in the park:
Dude, stagecoach tourist, either sex.
Dude heaver, lady tourist.
Sour dough tourist or
Sagebrusher, outdoor camper.
Swaddie, soldier.
Savage, stagecoach driver.
Skinner, driver of several horses or mules, especially a freighter.
Tackie, horse.
Barn dog, hostler.
Heaver, lady, especially a waitress.
Mulligan dump, drivers' mess.
Queen of the mulligan, waitress in drivers' mess.

The d e s i g n a t i o n "dude," which even antedated establishment of Western dude ranches, embodies respect and admiration; "tackie" is an affectionate name for a horse; and a "queen of the mulligan" was indeed regal. No disrespect is implied in any of the terms, old or current, of the characteristic Yellowstone lingo.

A peerless asset. It is certain that all who have visited Yellowstone National Park share with those who are constantly associated with it, the feeling that at all costs, the park should be preserved intact. It is an obligation of the people of today to those of tomorrow.

Not only the largest and most important geysers of the world, but the most extensive and varied collection of thermal features anywhere to be found, are in this park.

It is a place of sylvan beauty too—an incomparable sanctuary for wildlife—a wilderness of peaks, canyons, streams, falls and lakes, ever changing with the seasons; ever moving with the shadows.

It is Nature's shrine, where despoliation has been dispelled by wonderment.

Yet, however difficult it is to believe, there are a few otherwise good Americans always ready to foster projects that would seriously mar the natural beauty of the park itself, or damage its attractions. It has been necessary, ever since the establishment of this area as a national park, to maintain an unceasing defense of the park against attempts to utilize its peerless assets for commercial advantage.

Some proposals in the past, which have seemed entirely harmless, have met defeat on the ground that as insidious entering wedges they may threaten the sanctity of this region, one of the few remaining wilderness areas of the United States.

It is the common duty, not only of the citizens of the states adjacent to Yellowstone Park, whose interest is perhaps more material, but of the citizens of the entire country, all of whom have an equal proprietary interest in this great national park, to protect this asset through the delegations representing them in Congress, and in all other ways, from any form of encroachment. The diversion of its waters, any changes in its drainage, or any action that might destroy or tend to endanger its great natural scenic beauty, its diversified natural wildlife, or its world famous collection of mysterious and amazing thermal features, must be avoided.

Preventing desecration of the park, its natural features and man-made structures, is largely a responsibility of park visitors. Among the large number there are always a few thoughtless people who seek to immortalize themselves by inscribing their names at every opportunity, those who seem unable to resist the urge to throw things into the hot springs and craters, and those who endanger the lives of others by rolling rocks down the sides of the mountains and canyons, without thinking that possibly fishermen or picnickers in their direct paths, or the paths of avalanches sometimes just that easily started.

Early visitors to the park used pine boughs for mattresses, picked all the wild flowers they wanted, collected specimens of the formations which took years to develop, set fire to grass and started forest fires by their careless use of fire, walked on fragile formations

YELLOWSTONE PARK BISON
COPYRIGHT HAYNES INC.

that crunched and broke beneath their feet, shot animals whenever they wanted meat, heads or hides, and in other ways desecrated the area.

On May 7, 1894, all hunting was abruptly stopped within the park by the enactment of laws carrying heavy penalties for poaching. The force protecting the park has been enlarged from time to time, but even now it is not reasonable to expect the law enforcement agencies to stop all of the willful or thoughtless destruction or desecration of park features.

Since the park is owned by the people it is natural to expect them to take as great an interest in the prevention of damage and destruction as do the authorities, whose duty it is to enforce the rules, regulations, and laws within the park.

The Grand Loop Road of the Park name, was first suggested in 1923 by Harry W. Frantz, who at that time wrote:

"Gravel and bridges and engineering skill alone do not make a great road. The footprints and the hoofmarks and, if you will, the tire prints of countless travelers are required. And, too, the road must lead somewhere—to a mosque, to a shrine, to a sacred river, to Tartary or to Mecca.

"Slowly but as certainly as mathematics The Grand Loop Road of Yellowstone Park is becoming a great national highway. It is a road entwined in the lives and the dreams of an ever-growing number of people, the path of pilgrims seeking the God of the Open Air. About it, too, there accumulates a great volume of tradition—the passing of Presidents and Princes, the meetings of poets and peasants."

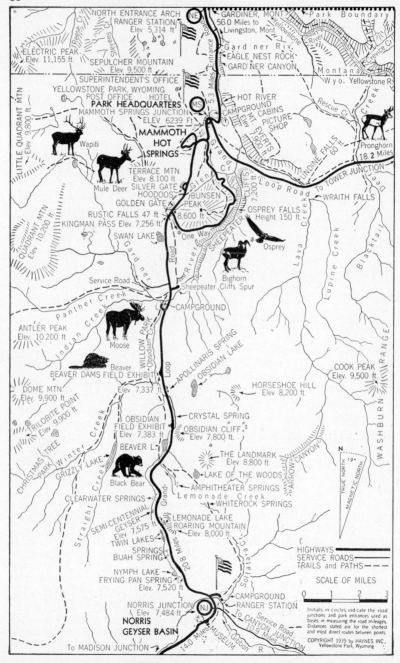

NORTH ENTRANCE ARCH
RANGER STATION
Elev. 5,314 ft
NE

GARDINER, MONT
56.0 Miles to
Livingston, Mont

Park Boundary

ELECTRIC PEAK
Elev. 11,155 ft.

SEPULCHER MOUNTAIN
Elev. 9,500 ft.

Gardner Riv.
EAGLE NEST ROCK
GARDNER CANYON

Montana
Wyo. Yellowstone R.

SUPERINTENDENT'S OFFICE
YELLOWSTONE PARK, WYOMING
POST OFFICE HOTEL
PARK HEADQUARTERS
MAMMOTH SPRINGS JUNCTION
ELEV. 6239 Ft.
MS

HOT RIVER
CAMPGROUND
MT. CABINS
PICTURE
SHOP

MT. EVERTS
Elev. 7,900 ft.

LITTLE QUADRANT MTN
Elev. 9,800 ft.

**MAMMOTH
HOT
SPRINGS**

Wapiti

Mule Deer

TERRACE MTN
Elev. 8,100 ft
SILVER GATE
HOODOOS
GOLDEN GATE

RUSTIC FALLS 47 ft
KINGMAN PASS Elev. 7,256 ft

QUADRANT MTN
Elev. 10,200 ft

BUNSEN
PEAK
8,600 ft.

Glen Cr.

UNDINE FALLS 60 ft.

Loop Road To TOWER JUNCTION

Pronghorn
18.2 Miles

WRAITH FALLS

OSPREY FALLS
Height 150 ft.

One Way
SHEEPEATER

Osprey

SWAN LAKE

Gardner

Service Road

Panther Creek

Indian Creek

ANTLER PEAK
Elev. 10,200 ft.

Moose

Beaver

BEAVER DAMS FIELD EXHIBIT

Bighorn
Sheepeater Cliffs Spur

CAMPGROUND

WILLOW PARK
Obsidian Cr.

Loop

APOLLINARIS SPRING
OBSIDIAN LAKE

Elev. 7,337 ft

HORSESHOE HILL
Elev. 8,200 ft.

COOK PEAK
Elev. 9,500 ft.

Lava Creek

Lupine Creek

Blacktail

WASHBURN RANGE

DOME MTN.
Elev. 9,900 ft.

TRILOBITE POINT
Elev. 9,900 ft.

Christmas Tree

Park Winter Creek

GRIZZLY LAKE

OBSIDIAN
FIELD EXHIBIT
Elev. 7,383 ft

BEAVER L.

Black Bear

CLEARWATER SPRINGS

Straight Creek

SEMI-CENTENNIAL
GEYSER
Elev. 7,575 ft
TWIN LAKES

SPRINGS
BIJAH SPRING

NYMPH LAKE
FRYING PAN SPRING
Elev. 7,520 ft

CRYSTAL SPRING

OBSIDIAN CLIFF
Elev. 7,800 ft.

THE LANDMARK
Elev. 8,800 ft.

LAKE OF THE WOODS

AMPHITHEATER SPRINGS
Lemonade Creek
WHITEROCK SPRINGS

LEMONADE LAKE
ROARING MOUNTAIN
Elev. 8,000 ft.

ARROW CANYON

Grand

Solfatara Cr.

NORRIS JUNCTION
Elev. 7,484 ft
NJ

**NORRIS
GEYSER BASIN**

To MADISON JUNCTION

CAMPGROUND
RANGER STATION

To CANYON JUNCTION
10.9 Miles

Service Road

MUSEUM

Gibbon R.

N
TRUE NORTH
MAGNETIC NORTH
19°

HIGHWAYS ———
SERVICE ROADS — — —
TRAILS and PATHS ---

SCALE OF MILES
0   1   2   3

Initials in circles indicate the road
junctions and park entrances used as
bases in measuring the road mileages.
Distances stated are for the shortest
and most direct routes between points

COPYRIGHT 1939 by HAYNES INC.
Yellowstone Park, Wyoming

POINTS of INTEREST

with descriptions which include distances and elevations, plant and animal life, geology, history, services and accommodations.

NORTH ENTRANCE

Gardiner, Montana, just outside the northern boundary of the park, not only supplies the needs of ranchers and the miners and their families at the gold and arsenic mines, and travertine rock q u a r - ries nearby, but also caters to park visitors from early spring until late fall when snow closes all park roads excepting the 5.3 mile stretch from Gardiner to park headquarters at Mammoth, and the 48.2 mile stretch from Mammoth via Tower Junction to the Northeast Entrance over which snowplows are operated. Gardiner serves operators and guests of nearby dude ranches, and hunters many of whom come from great distances to hunt in season, in the mountainous area outside the park. In the early days Gardiner was the outfitting station for horseback expeditions into the park. Now are gone the hitching rack, the barn and blacksmith. Only old-timers recall the "Gee" and "Haw" of animal-drawn freight.

Gardiner Station, terminus of the park branch of the Northern Pacific Railway is near the Theodore Roosevelt Arch. Construction of the Northern Pacific Railway was begun in Minnesota in 1870, two years prior to the establishment of the park. Track-laying from Livingston, Montana Territory, was started southward up the Yellowstone River toward the park in 1882 past Yellowstone City, a frontier mining camp in Emigrant Gulch, and through Yankee Jim Canyon to the pioneer hamlet of Cinnabar which it reached on August 31, 1883. To get to Cinnabar the railroad had to buy out Yankee Jim, (James George), frontiersman who had built 27 miles of toll road through the only available pass in that district. Cinnabar was named for the bright red stone in nearby Devils Slide believed to be cinnabar (mercuric sulphide) ore, but in reality only colored stone. In 1902 the railroad was extended a distance of three miles from Cinnabar to Gardiner at the park boundary and was the first railroad to reach a park gateway. The rustic depot designed by the late Robert C. Reamer had hardly reached completion in Gardiner before Cinnabar had reverted to prairie. (Park buses connect with all trains during the summer season.) The road to Livingston, Montana, about 56 miles north of Gardiner, crosses a recently constructed steel and concrete bridge over the Yellowstone River in Gardiner and continues to within a short distance of Livingston on the east side of the river. The old wagon road and the railroad are on the west side all the way.

The North Entrance (Gardiner) may be reached via Northwest Airlines from Chicago and the Twin Cities (Minneapolis-Saint Paul) to Billings, Montana, or from North Pacific Coast points, to Butte, Montana, thence via the Northern Pacific Railway to Gardiner.

NORTH ENTRANCE
to
MAMMOTH HOT SPRINGS

This 5.3 mile entrance road joins The Grand Loop Road of the Park at Mammoth Springs Junction.

High lights are the historically important area near the junction of the Yellowstone and Gardner rivers, the scenic and geological aspects of Gardner Canyon and the foothills and mountains, and the remarkable wild life ranges and vegetation of comparatively low elevations through the rise of nearly a thousand feet attained in the 5.3 mile drive from the entrance to Mammoth.

(NOTE: The first distance figure shown at the beginning of key paragraphs, applies to those traveling in the same direction as the sequence of paragraphs. Those traveling in the opposite direction, read the paragraphs in reverse order and use the second, instead of the first, distance figure.)

THEODORE ROOSEVELT ARCH

0.00   5.30   **T h e o d o r e Roosevelt Arch** at the north boundary, elevation 5,314 ft. The arch designed and built under the supervision of Maj. H. M. Chittenden, Corps of Engineers, U. S. Army, was dedicated by President Theodore Roosevelt on April 24, 1903. It bears the inscription "For the Benefit and Enjoyment of the People" quoted from the Act of Dedication of the park (March 1, 1872). **National Park Service** rangers at the checking stations here as at all park entrances record all vehicles entering and leaving the park, and issue season permits upon payment of the motor vehicle license fees prescribed by the Secretary of the Interior. F i r e a r m s are sealed. Dogs are permitted in the park but must be kept on leash or in crates. Upon leaving the park all visitors are requested to report the number of fish caught.

Fish and Fishing. In the Yellowstone and Gardner rivers and other waters near the North Entrance are the cutthroat trout (redthroat, blackspotted, native), rainbow, Loch L e v e n and eastern b r o o k (speckled) trout; and in the Yellowstone River are some whitefish. Fishing licenses are required in the three states adjoining the park, but within its boundaries none is required.

Reptiles are rare in the park. It is a comforting fact that the rattlesnake is not found above 6,000 feet elevation and practically the entire park is considerably above the zones of poisonous reptiles.

0.10   5.20   **Pronghorns** (antelope) are seen frequently on the grazing ground on either side of the road. These keeneyed wild animals, fleet of foot and timid, are preserved in their natural state in but few places in the U. S. Unlike the wapiti (elk), deer and moose the pronghorn is armed with hollow horns like those of cattle, but unlike cattle they shed their horns each year, a long, pointed bony horn core covered by the undeveloped new horn always remaining. The horns are present in both sexes. **Photographing** these animals is a fascinating sport and usually successful when one approaches them slowly and silently to within "shooting" distance. (Rapid movements, slamming automobile doors, talking and any other distraction should be avoided).

Electric Peak (11,155 ft.), second highest mountain in the park, is the pointed peak seven miles southwest. (Eagle Peak near the southeast corner of the park is its highest one—11,360 ft.) When traveling toward Mammoth, Electric Peak is in the right, rear distance; **Sheep Mtn.** (10,628 ft.) at left rear— a peak of the Snowy Range outside of the park; **Sepulcher Mtn.** (9,500 ft.) named "because of a tomb-like rock" on its northwest slope is at right. The structures at the left are the garage, repair shops, commissary and quarters for employees of the Yellowstone Park Company.

0.45   4.85   J u n c t i o n. Service road to buildings of Y. P. Co. The opposite side road is the old road (4.2 miles) to Mammoth used by " g a m e stalkers". Visitors are advised to drive over this old, steep and narrow road in the direction from Mammoth toward the North Entrance, rather than in the reverse direction, thus avoiding, to a large extent, meeting other cars.

0.60   4.70   The **Gardner River** seen at north, enters the Yellowstone River about a half mile away. Excepting only the name "Yellowstone", Gardner is the oldest name in the entire park region. It dates back to 1832 to a free trader and trapper named Johnson Gardner (not Gardiner), who trapped for the American Fur Company post at Fort Union. It was near this junction that on August 25,

1870, two years before the park was established, the famous **Expedition of 1870** camped after following a trail up the Yellowstone along which most of that day were the marks on both sides of lodgepoles dragged in the sand. Indians had preceded the party. That night on distant hills were signal fires which made known the presence of men destined not only to explore this marvelous region, but to conceive and bring to fruition the national park idea, and the establishment of Yellowstone National Park (Mar. 1, 1872). The route taken by this party up the Yellowstone River back of Mt. Everts and across Blacktail Deer and Tower creeks was part of the **Great Trail** of the Indians, which at many places even today is still in evidence.

0.80   4.50   The old **target range** across the Gardner River was used by the U. S. Army during part of the period (1886-1916) when the administration of the park was vested in the military, and the commanding officers at Fort Yellowstone (Mammoth) were detailed as acting superintendents. Since 1916, when the National Park Service was established, it has administered the park and the superintendents have been civilians.

Sepulcher Mountain is again in view from this point.

1.10   4.20   North end of **Gardner Canyon.** Along the roadsides are cedar trees (Juniperus scopulorum) and other

EAGLE NEST ROCK
(OSPREY'S NEST)

evergreens. The principal shrubs are the sagebrush (Artemisia tridentata) and greasewood (Sarcobatus). Near the river are shrubby willows.

1.50   3.80   A view of **Eagle Nest Rock** ahead across the river may be had by travelers enroute to Mammoth. The nest of the osprey (fish hawk) on the summit of the pinnacle is five feet across and is inhabited every year.

1.60   3.70   Gardner River crossing. Those enroute to the North Entrance view Eagle Nest Rock at right shortly before crossing the river.

1.85   3.45   The stratified cliffs above the road are sedimentary, fossil-bearing marine deposits of the Cretaceous period. Across the river is a **Sliding Hill.** The broken ground extends up the foothills of Sepulcher Mountain for more than a mile. As fast as the earth is forced into the river it is carried away. In this vicinity bighorns (mountain sheep) are sometimes seen from the road, especially in the late fall and early spring.

2.60   2.70   South end of **Gardner Canyon.**

On the foothills the pronghorns and mule deer are not infrequently seen in summer; and w a p i t i roam these hills in spring and fall.

3.00   2.30   Gardner River crossing. Above this point is a typical glacial valley. Glacial moraines cover several square miles of terrain between Mt. Everts, Bunsen Peak, Sepulcher Mountain, a n d t h e North Entrance.

The **umbrella plant** (Eriogonum), also known as wild buckwheat, grows in the open dry places, often being part of the undergrowth among the sagebrush. It occurs in several species throughout the park and blooms the greater part of the summer, having very small white flowers. It is called "umbrella plant" because of the shape of the cluster of flowers.

Sagebrush (Artemisia) occurs in the park in several species, most common of which is "tridentata," the variety with the three-prong leaf, which grows 2 or 3 feet high, but around Mammoth some exceptionally large bushes nearly 10 feet in height are not uncommon. This is the typical gray bush of the

EAGLE NEST ROCK IN
GARDNER CANYON

Western plains, which is dustcolored and distinctly fragrant. Before the days of resident physicians and nurses in the park, when remedies of the mountain men were more in vogue than today, the so-called mountain fever was treated by the patient drinking much of the bitter tea steeped from the dried leaves of this otherwise almost useless plant.

Pricklypear cactus (Opuntia), growing only in dry places, is usually associated with the sagebrush at lower elevations in the park. Its principal characteristic is the great number of sharp spines that grow in clusters from the flat, fleshy, somewhat rounded joints, sometimes called leaves, of this plant. Its flowers are quite large and exceptionally beautiful varying from yellow to purplish on the outside with orange centers. It is said that plainsmen in the prairie country used the juice s q u e e z e d from these fleshy joints to make the alkali water more palatable and safe to drink. During hard winters, wapiti and pronghorns feed on cactus.

3.10   2.20   **M o n t a n a -Wyoming State Line**, 45° north latitude, crossing. In general this line parallels the northern park boundary which is a little more than two miles to the north. Rising m o r e t h a n 2,000 feet above the Gardner River to the east, is **Mt. Everts** (7,900 ft.), a cliff composed chiefly of fossil-bearing marine deposits (Cretaceous). Intrusions of andesite porphyry are seen near the north end high above the low slopes where several coal seams have been found. The heavy cap of rhyolite porphyry extends almost three miles along its crest. Truman C. Everts for whom this mountain was named, was the member of the Expedition of 1870 who became separated from the party and was found 37 days later emaciated and barely alive on a knoll about 8 miles east of Mammoth by **Jack Baronett and George Pritchett**.

Stickleaf (Mentzelia), one of the rarest and most beautiful wild flowers in the entire region, occurs in desolate, arid places at elevations of 6,000 feet or less and blooms only in the evening and at night, when it exhales a rich, heavy perfume. In the daytime it resembles a thistle. Its name is derived from the fact that its lance-shaped leaves are covered with tiny hooked bristles that cling to anything they touch. Flowers, which are seen during July and August, are 3 to 5 inches in diameter with usually 5 to 10 light yellow petals and many long yellow stamens.

3.60   1.70   Steam rising from **Hot River** may be seen on the near bank of Gardner River at the foot of Mt. Everts. It is 6 to 8 feet wide and issues from a rock ledge near the river. Many observers believe that this hot stream flows for a considerable distance underground and drains all or part of the Mammoth Hot Springs area.

4.00   1.30   **Bunsen Peak** (8,600 ft.), for those enroute to Mammoth, is directly ahead at a distance of 3½ miles. It was named for Robert Wilhelm Bunsen, eminent German physicist who studied geysers in Iceland and evolved a geyser theory which for a long time was generally accepted.

4.30   1.00   **Mammoth Campground** occupies the area between here and—

4.60   0.70   where there are camp sites, cabins, cafeteria, grocery, picture shop, rest rooms, etc.

4.90   0.40   The road is cut through ancient travertine —calcium carbonate rock— which was deposited by hot springs.

5.30   0.00   **Mammoth Springs Junction.** Elevation 6,239 ft. This junction, marked by the flagpole in front of the superintendent's office, is the approximate center of Mammoth, administrative headquarters of the park on The Grand Loop Road of the Park.

MAMMOTH HOT SPRINGS

Mammoth (P. O. Yellowstone Park, Wyo.), the village at park headquarters at Mammoth Hot Springs, has the largest resident population of any in the park, and is the only year-round community. The road to the North Entrance has always been kept open throughout the year; snowplows were first used regularly to the Northeast Entrance via Tower Junction during the winter of 1938-9. All other park roads are open only from early spring to late fall.

The office of Park Superintendent, the U. S. Post Office, and U. S. Commissioner's office function the year-round. Winter or summer offices of all of park concessioners (concerns serving the public under government franchises) also receive mail addressed to Yellowstone Park, Wyoming, at any time of year.

Mammoth has been developed both by the government and the park concessioners, in three rather distinct areas at different elevations.

The first is the flat on which are most of the structures, including the superintendent's office at the Junction (Elev. 6,239 ft.), at the east of which are the repair shop and garage, and post office; at west are Mammoth Springs Hotel (also headquarters of the Yellowstone Park Company), cottages, dining room and Terrace Grill, general store, filling station, Park Curio Shop and coffee shop (also including headquarters of Mesdames Pryor & Trischman), and the U. S. Commissioner's office. At the southeast are the museum and information office, picture shop (also headquarters of Haynes Inc.) and (at about 0.4 mile on the Mammoth-Tower Fall Road) the chapel and hospital (also headquarters of the park physician), and the Amphitheater for evening lectures.

The second area (0.7 to 1.0 mile, on the North Entrance Road), at from 100 to 200 feet lower elevations, embraces the campground and camp sites, cabins, cafeteria, grocery, picture shop, etc.

The third area (0.7 to 0.8 mile on the Mammoth-Norris Road), at about 100 feet higher elevation, has the swimming pool.

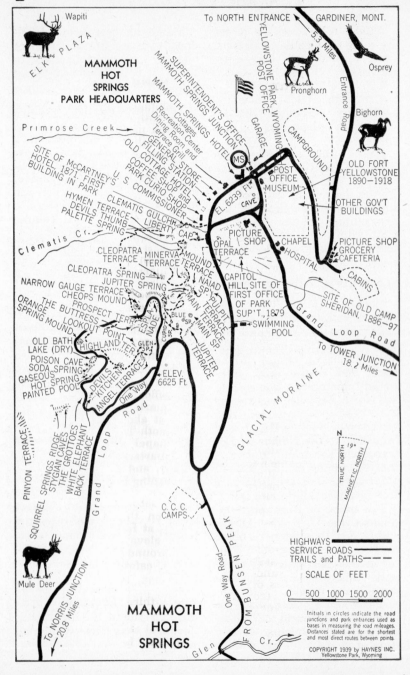

MAMMOTH
HOT
SPRINGS PARK HEADQUARTERS

Wapiti

ELK PLAZA

To NORTH ENTRANCE — GARDINER, MONT.

5.3 Miles

Osprey

Pronghorn

Bighorn

Primrose Creek

SUPERINTENDENT'S OFFICE
MAMMOTH SPRINGS JUNCTION
MAMMOTH SPRINGS HOTEL
Mammoth Cottages
Recreation Center
Dining Room and Terrace Grill

YELLOWSTONE PARK, WYOMING
POST OFFICE

Entrance Road

GARAGE

CAMPGROUND

OLD FORT
YELLOWSTONE
1890-1918

SITE OF McCARTNEY'S
HOTEL, 1871, FIRST
BUILDING IN PARK

U.S. COMMISSIONER
PARK CURIO SHOP
COFFEE SHOP
OLD COTTAGE HOTEL
FILLING STATION
GENERAL STORE

MS

EL. 6239 FT.

POST
OFFICE
MUSEUM

OTHER GOV'T
BUILDINGS

HYMEN TERRACE
DEVILS THUMB
PALETTE SPRING

CLEMATIS GULCH
LIBERTY CAP

CAVE

PICTURE SHOP

CHAPEL

PICTURE SHOP
GROCERY
CAFETERIA

Clematis Cr.

CLEOPATRA
TERRACE

MINERVA
TERRACE

MOUND
TERRACE

OPAL
TERRACE

HOSPITAL

CABINS

CLEOPATRA SPRING
JUPITER SPRING
NARROW GAUGE TERRACE
CHEOPS MOUND
THE BUTTRESS
PROSPECT TERRACE
ORANGE
SPRING MOUND
LOOKOUT POINT

NAIAD
SP.

ESPLANADE

MAIN TERRACE

PULPIT TERRACE

CAPITOL
HILL, SITE OF
FIRST OFFICE
OF PARK
SUP'T, 1879

SITE OF OLD CAMP
SHERIDAN, 1886-97

BLUE
SP.

MAIN SP.

SWIMMING
POOL

Grand Loop Road

To TOWER JUNCTION
18.2 Miles

OLD BATH
LAKE (DRY)
POISON CAVE
SODA SPRING
GASEOUS
HOT SPRING
PAINTED POOL

HIGHLAND TER.

GLEN
SP.

CUPID SP.

DEVILS
KITCHEN
ANGEL TERRACE

JUPITER
TERRACE

ELEV.
6625 Ft.

One Way

GLACIAL MORAINE

Road

PINYON TERRACE

SQUIRREL SPRINGS RIDGE
STYGIAN CAVES
THE GROTTOES
WHITE ELEPHANT
BACK TERRACE

Grand Loop Road

C.C.C.
CAMPS

Mule Deer

To NORRIS JUNCTION
20.8 Miles

One Way Road

FROM BUNSEN PEAK

Glen Cr.

N

TRUE NORTH
19°
MAGNETIC NORTH

HIGHWAYS
SERVICE ROADS
TRAILS and PATHS

SCALE OF FEET

0   500 1000 1500 2000

Initials in circles indicate the road
junctions and park entrances used as
bases in measuring the road mileages.
Distances stated are for the shortest
and most direct routes between points.

MAMMOTH
HOT
SPRINGS

Settlement in what is now the park began at Mammoth in 1871 when James C. McCartney built a log cabin hotel in Clematis Gulch west of Liberty Cap; and M a t t h e w McGuirk built a cabin near Hot River on the old wagon road connecting the area near the junction of the Gardner and Yellowstone rivers with Cooke, Montana Territory, a mining camp just outside the present northeast corner of the park (both were razed). The first superintendent's o f f i c e was built on the summit of Capitol Hill by Superintendent P. W. Norris in 1879 (razed in 1909). In the year 1884, Frank Jay H a y n e s, park photographer, built his first park studio and picture shop on the flat facing M a m m o t h Hotel (razed in 1928). In 1885 the Cottage Hotel (now used only as a dormitory) was built by Walter and Helen L. Henderson. Camp Sheridan, between Jupiter Terrace and Capitol Hill, was established in 1886 and abandoned in 1897 (now razed). Construction of Fort Yellowstone was begun in 1890, and it was later much enlarged. In 1916, when the park administration was taken over by the National Park Service, the former fort and all its buildings were transferred to it.

Some of the present day structures with the dates of their erection are recorded as follows: superintendent's office (1903), hospital (1911), chapel (1913), picture shop in campground (1927), p i c t u r e shop and headquarters (1929), post office (1937). Mammoth Springs Hotel (1937).

A large number of the buildings at Mammoth are used for housing the officers and personnel, and for shops and storage of records, equipment and merchandise of both the government and park concessioners.

The old road to the North Entrance, used by "game stalkers" is the sidehill road back of the superintendent's office.

MAMMOTH HOT SPRINGS
to
NORRIS GEYSER BASIN

0.00   20.80   **Mammoth Springs Junction,** elevation 6,-239 ft., where the North Entrance Road joins The Grand Loop Road, is marked by the flagpole in front of the office of the superintendent of Yellowstone National Park.

0.10   20.70   **Mammoth Springs Hotel** is composed of a group of buildings, one housing the general offices and lounge, back of which is the recreation center building and a group of furnished cottages. The large wing attached t o t h e m a i n building is equipped with hotel rooms. The other building on the main street is the main dining-room, at the far end of which is the Terrace Grill.

Construction o f t h e f i r s t Mammoth Springs Hotel on this site was begun in 1883 and was completed in 1886. This old building was razed in 1936.

MAMMOTH SPRINGS HOTEL

0.15   20.65   **General Store.**
This store, open the year round
and the filling-station just
beyond, are operated by Pryor
and Trischman.

0.25   20.55   **Park Curio
Shop** and coffee shop, operated
by Pryor and Trischman, are
housed in the building just beyond the old Cottage Hotel.

The stone building in Clematis Gulch is the office of the
United States Commissioner.

Hymen Terrace, near the
road, is very active at some
seasons while at other times
the springs are dry and the terrace then loses its brilliant colorings, as has been the case for
the past few seasons.

0.30   20.50   **Liberty Cap**
is an extinct hot spring cone,
37 feet high and 20 feet in diameter at its base. It is formed by
over-lapping layers of travertine (calcium carbonate).

Opal Terrace at the foot of
Capitol Hill, ahead, is one of the
more rapidly depositing formations.

Haynes Picture Shop and
headquarters of Haynes Inc. is
down the road about 300 yards
beyond several residences of
park concessioners. Beyond this
building are the residences of
the government personnel, the
museum, hospital, and chapel.

Capitol Hill, elevation 6,420
ft., a glacial moraine, rises 145
feet above the road at this
point. On top of this hill, the
first superintendent's office was
built in 1879 (razed in 1909).
It was in a sense a fort as it
had a bullet-proof cupola,
deemed necessary as the Indians were still hostile at that
time. The incursions into the
park by the Nez Perce and
Bannock Indians occurred in
1877 and 1878.

0.45   20.35   On the lower
slope of Terrace Mountain, opposite Capitol Hill, is conspicuous **Mound Terrace,** beyond
which on the level of its summit is **Naiad Spring,** while below at its right are **Minerva**
and **Cleopatra** terraces.

0.70   20.10   **Mammoth
Swimming Pool** of natural
warm water from nearby terraces, is east of Jupiter Terrace. In the opposite direction
may be seen the 2,000 foot cliff
of Mt. Everts, composed chiefly
of fossil-bearing sandstone and

JUPITER TERRACE

shale; the igneous rocks of this cliff are a heavy and extensive cap of rhyolite porphyry and at the northern end, intrusions of andesite porphyry. The valley of Lava Creek is at the east between Mt. Everts and Sheepeater Cliffs, beyond which may be seen Prospect Peak (9,300 ft.), the most northerly summit of the Washburn Range.

0.85   19.95   **Jupiter Terrace.** The white or gray hill of calcareous hot spring deposit was formed by the waters of the large hot springs near its crest. Where the waters flow the algal coloring is conspicuous. The group of shelflike formations was named **Pulpit**

Terrace, when active a number of years ago.

1.10   19.70   On both sides of the road are glacial deposits which were spread over most of the valley and extend to the south and east for many miles.

1.30   19.50   **Bunsen Peak Loop Road** which takes off from the main road on Swan Lake Flat, 3.6 miles south, enters the main road at this point; it is a one-way road which may not be driven from this end.

1.40   19.40   About a hundred yards northeast of the road is a cold spring, which in the early days marked the site of a favorite camping ground.

1.60   19.20   To the north is seen the pointed S h e e p Mountain (10,628 ft.) in the Snowy Range beyond the park boundary.

1.90   18.90   **Main Terrace.** The Terrace Trail meets the road here. One should visit Cupid Spring, Blue Spring, and Main Spring on this terrace. Sepulcher Mtn. (9,500 ft.) is seen in the distance beyond the terraces.

2.10   18.70   **Terrace Loop Junction,** elevation 6,625 ft. This loop, 1.6 miles in length, connects at several points with the Terrace Trail. Among the points of interest on this loop are: The Esplanade (f r o m which a fine view of the village of Mammoth may be had), **Narrow Gauge Terrace, Cheops Mound, The Buttress, Orange Spring Mound, Old Bath Lake,**

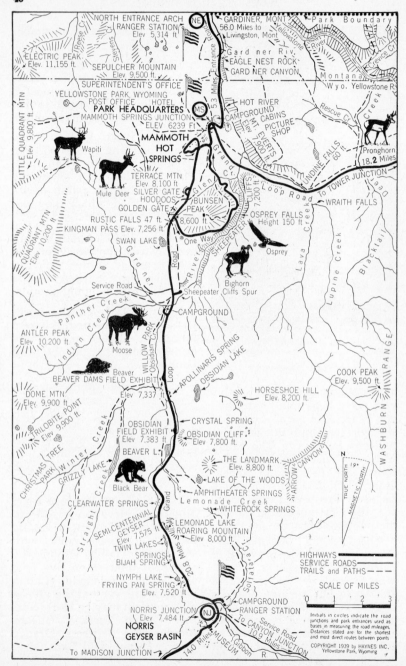

NORTH ENTRANCE ARCH
RANGER STATION
Elev. 5,314 ft.

GARDINER, MONT.
56.0 Miles to
Livingston, Mont.

Park Boundary

ELECTRIC PEAK
Elev. 11,155 ft.

SEPULCHER MOUNTAIN
Elev. 9,500 ft.

Gardner Riv.
EAGLE NEST ROCK
GARDNER CANYON

Montana
Wyo. Yellowstone R.

SUPERINTENDENT'S OFFICE
YELLOWSTONE PARK, WYOMING
POST OFFICE   HOTEL
PARK HEADQUARTERS
MAMMOTH SPRINGS JUNCTION
ELEV 6239 Ft.

HOT RIVER
CAMPGROUND
MT. EVERTS
Elev. 7,900 ft.
CABINS
PICTURE
SHOP

MAMMOTH
HOT
SPRINGS

Wapiti

UNDINE FALLS
60 ft.

Pronghorn
18.2 Miles

LITTLE QUADRANT MTN
Elev. 9,800 ft.

TERRACE MTN
Elev. 8,100 ft.
Mule Deer SILVER GATE
HOODOOS
GOLDEN GATE
RUSTIC FALLS 47 ft.
KINGMAN PASS Elev. 7,256 ft.
SWAN LAKE

To TOWER JUNCTION
Loop Road
WRAITH FALLS

QUADRANT MTN
Elev. 10,200 ft.

BUNSEN
PEAK
8,600 ft.

OSPREY FALLS
Height 150 ft.

One Way
SHEEPEATER CLIFFS

Osprey

Service Road

Sheepeater Cliffs Spur

Bighorn

CAMPGROUND

Panther Creek

ANTLER PEAK
Elev. 10,200 ft.

Moose

APOLLINARIS SPRING
OBSIDIAN LAKE

COOK PEAK
Elev. 9,500 ft.

Beaver
BEAVER DAMS FIELD EXHIBIT
Elev. 7,337 ft.

HORSESHOE HILL
Elev. 8,200 ft.

DOME MTN
Elev. 9,900 ft.

CRYSTAL SPRING

TRILOBITE POINT
Elev. 9,900 ft.

OBSIDIAN
FIELD EXHIBIT
Elev. 7,383 ft.

OBSIDIAN CLIFF
Elev. 7,800 ft.

CHRISTMAS
TREE
PARK

BEAVER L.

THE LANDMARK
Elev. 8,800 ft.
LAKE OF THE WOODS

GRIZZLY LAKE

Black Bear

AMPHITHEATER SPRINGS

CLEARWATER SPRINGS

Lemonade Creek

WHITEROCK SPRINGS

SEMI-CENTENNIAL
GEYSER
Elev. 7,575 ft.
TWIN LAKES
SPRINGS
BIJAH SPRING

LEMONADE LAKE
ROARING MOUNTAIN
Elev. 8,000 ft.

NYMPH LAKE
FRYING PAN SPRING
Elev. 7,520 ft.

HIGHWAYS
SERVICE ROADS
TRAILS and PATHS - - -

SCALE OF MILES

0   1   2   3

NORRIS JUNCTION
Elev. 7,484 ft.

CAMPGROUND
RANGER STATION

NORRIS
GEYSER BASIN

To CANYON JUNCTION
10.9 Miles

Initials in circles indicate the road
junctions and park entrances used as
bases in measuring the road mileages.
Distances stated are for the shortest
and most direct routes between points

COPYRIGHT 1939 by HAYNES INC.
Yellowstone Park, Wyoming

To MADISON JUNCTION
14.0 Miles

TRUE NORTH
MAGNETIC NORTH
19°

WASHBURN RANGE

TERRACES ATOP JUPITER TERRACE

Poison Cave, Devils Kitchen, Stygian Caves, White Elephant Back Terrace, and Angel Terrace. **Poison Cave**, with an orifice about two feet across is filled with deadly v o l c a n i c gases which cause the eyes to smart even while leaning over to look into its chamber. Any animals or birds seeking shelter here would surely lose their lives. **Devils Kitchen**, the interior of an extinct hot spring, about 35 feet deep and 75 feet in length, is typical of the caverns common to many active hot springs in this region. A stairway into this cavern was removed (1939) on account of the danger to visitors due to the presence of carbon dioxide. **Stygian Caves**, at the foot of

Squirrel Springs Ridge **are** about 200 yards west of White Elephant Back Terrace. **Stygian** (hellish; infernal; deathly) **Caves** seem to have been appropriately named due to the poisonous or suffocating gases which issue from low openings and kill small birds and animals which enter them.

The **mule deer**, of which the estimate is 700, are widely distributed throughout the park. Its color is brown in summer and steel-gray in winter; the average weight of the adult buck is 200 pounds; the mating season is November and December; and fawns, usually one but occasionally twins, are born in May and June. Antlers, borne only by the buck (al-

TWIN MULE DEER FAWNS

though one case of a doe with antlers was reported repeatedly in the Tower Fall area) attain full growth in August or September and are shed in February or March. The antlers when first formed are soft and are each shaped like two Y's, one below the other, and joined together, and they are covered with a downy velvet which later wears or is rubbed off. The main stem of the antlers is called the beam and the pointed branches are tines or points, while the antlers of the young bucks are called spikes.

Like the young of many other species of wild animals in the park, the mule deer fawn has a protective coloration and camouflage spots, which, with the instinctive habit of lying motionless that characterizes the young of many species, protect it from friendly park visitors as well as its natural enemies.

2.50   18.30   **Snow Pass Trail.** Snow Pass, elevation 7,450 ft., is between Clagett Butte and Terrace Mountain, about two miles from Mammoth on the first road ever built from Mammoth to Swan Lake Flat. It was used in the days of the stage coaches before t h e present Kingman P a s s (Golden Gate) road was built.

3.75   17.05   **Silver Gate** is visited by a very short one-way loop road. This was one of the attractions in the Hoodoos on the former highway. The **Hoodoos,** which extend for about one-half mile on both sides of the road, are huge blocks of ancient travertine, deposited in pre-glacial times by hot springs. The present tumbled position of this large mass of blocks is due to a huge landslide on the flank of Terrace Mountain.

Larkspur (Delphinium) derives its name from "Delphin," in allusion to the shape of the flower, which is not unlike the classic dolphin. The tall species (particularly the seeds) of

BUNSEN PEAK FROM GRAND LOOP ROAD

this dark blue flower is very poisonous and throughout the Rockies causes great loss to stockmen raising grazing animals.

4.50   16.30   Golden Gate, north end, is marked by a large natural pillar; a smaller one is a little to the south at the end of the concrete viaduct. Golden Gate was so named on account of the yellow l i c h e n growing on the cliff. Bunsen Peak (8,600 ft.), composed of dacite porphyry, forms the opposite wall of Golden G a t e Canyon; the vertical escarpment on its face is called **Cathedral Rock.**

4.60   16.20   This observation point is a favorite place f r o m w h i c h to photograph Golden Gate Canyon.

4.70   16.10   Rustic Falls of Glen Creek (47 ft. high) is seen at Kingman Pass at the head of Golden Gate Canyon.

4.80   16.00   Kingman Pass is at an elevation of 7,256 feet, which is more than a thousand feet higher than Mammoth.

Gardners Hole known for more than a century, extends from here to the Gallatin Range beyond the ridge at the west.

4.90   15.90   North edge of **Swan Lake Flat,** Glen Creek crossing, is the start of the 6.15 mile one-way side trip around Bunsen Peak. Fishing is not permitted in Glen Creek nor in nearby waters which together provide the water supply for the village of Mammoth.

GOLDEN GATE CANYON NEAR KINGMAN PASS

BUNSEN PEAK LOOP

A 6.15 mile side loop road which is one-way for 5.9 miles. (One should not attempt to take a trailer over this narrow mountain road. It is steep in places and has several hairpin turns.)

High lights of this side trip are the awesome gorge of the Sheepeater Canyon, 800 feet deep, at the head of which is the 150-foot Osprey Falls; and a panoramic view of the valley of the Gardner River and the great terraces and mountains surrounding Mammoth Hot Springs from a point nearly a thousand feet higher than the village.

0.00 **Junction** 4.9 miles south of Mammoth Springs Junction. Elevation is about 7,256 feet at start of side trip. (Beginning of one-way zone for vehicular travel.) Road rejoins The Grand Loop at a junction 1.3 miles south of Mammoth Springs Junction at an elevation of about 6,400 ft.

0.01 **Glen Creek** crossing. Fishing is not permitted in this creek, nor in nearby waters which together provide the water supply for the village of Mammoth.

0.10 Turn right. (Left side road ends in a gravel pit.) The summit of **Bunsen Peak** (8,600 ft.) and the fire lookout seen in left distance ahead are reached only by trail. This mountain is 1,345 feet higher than the road.

0.30 The **Gallatin Range**, including Electric Peak (11,155 ft.), is at right across Swan Lake Flat, in Gardners Hole.

0.85 A glacial lake and its larger neighbor hidden in the timber some distance beyond, both at right, are f a v o r i t e haunts of wild animals and waterfowl.

1.90 Beyond Sheepeater Canyon of the Gardner River, are the three northerly mountains of the Washburn Range 8 to 10 miles distant. Only the tip of Prospect Peak (9,300 ft.) is visible beyond an intervening eminence. The mountain south (right) of this peak is Folsom Peak (9,200 ft.); and at its right is Cook Peak (9,500 ft.), highest of the three. Cook and Folsom peaks were named for two f a m o u s prospector-explorers who visited the upper Yellowstone region the year before the Expedition of 1870.

2.30 The road enters a grove of quaking aspen trees, then a mixed stand, and finally a forest of pine and spruce.

3.20 **Picnic area,** elevation about 7,150 ft., (no water). Rest rooms at right. Trail to summit of Bunsen Peak (8,600 ft.) is seen at left. This trail parallels the road from here to Mammoth. The road ahead makes a winding, steep descent for a quarter of a mile. (Proceed slowly.)

3.45 An **observation p o i n t,** elevation about 6,900 ft., is at right; a trail leads from here to the bottom of the gorge. About a mile upstream is **Osprey Falls,** an 150-foot plunge of the Gardner River. Across the gorge are **Sheepeater Cliffs** which extend for about two miles below the falls and eastward up Lava Creek to Undine Falls. These cliffs were named by Superintendent (1877-1882) P. W. Norris for the Sheepeater Indians, one of whose "ancient and but recently deserted, secluded, unknown haunts" he discovered. **Bighorns** (Rocky Mountain sheep) still inhabit this region and travel over a well-worn trail which extends for more than a mile along the perilous rim of the opposite wall. Unlike the wapiti (American stag or elk) whose trails are a hundreds yards or more back from the rim, the bighorns apparently enjoy the scenery and the thrills of surmounting sheer precipices. Deer, moose and bear also live in the primitive area of Sheepeater Cliffs. The impressive **Sheepeater Canyon** which is nearly half a mile wide at this point was carved 600-800 feet deep in the hard volcanic rock through almost countless ages, largely by glacial and stream erosion. On its walls are seen columnar and fan-shaped patterns in the basalt, a comparatively recent lava. The underlying rock is rhyolite porphyry, much in evidence, although the principal mass of Bunsen Peak is dacite.

4.10 **Sheep Mountain** (10,628 ft.), in the right distance ahead, is part of the Snowy Range outside the park. Its summit is 10 miles away, and nearly six miles beyond the boundary.

Mount Everts (7,900 ft.), the facing cliff at right is composed mostly of marine sediments, some of which are fossil-bearing. The spur of Sheepeater Cliffs rising from the Gardner River is in the right foreground south of the Mammoth-Tower Fall highway. The river is nearly 900 feet below this point.

4.20 The tip of **Electric Peak** (11,155 ft.), six miles away, is seen ahead beyond **C l a g e t t Butte** (8,100 ft.). **Sepulcher Mountain** (9,500 ft.) is at the right of the butte. From here one may see the great terraces of Mammoth Hot Springs and the village.

4.35 Abrupt hairpin turn. A steep descent (driven in low gear) extends beyond this point for nearly a mile.

4.40 Sheepeater Cliffs (7,200 ft.) are in the distance ahead.

4.45 Abrupt hairpin turn.

4.90 **Cathedral Rock**, on the face of Bunsen Peak, is in the left distance ahead, at the left of **Terrace Mountain** (8,100 ft.) and the Hoodoos.

5.25 **Glen Creek** crossing.

5.55 Sign: B u n s e n Peak Trail.

5.90 End of one-way zone for vehicular travel.

6.15 **Junction** 1.3 miles south of Mammoth Springs Junction. Elevation is about 6,400 ft. at end of side trip.

(NOTE: For continuation to Norris Geyser Basin, please turn back to distance 1.30 on page 45.)

ELECTRIC PEAK FROM BUNSEN PEAK

GRAND LOOP ROAD

5.10   15.70 Beyond Swan Lake Flat in Gardners Hole (west) is the **Gallatin Range.** Notable peaks left to right, are: Trilobite Point (9,900 ft.); Mt. Holmes, with a fire lookout on its 10,300 foot summit; Dome Mountain (9,900 ft.), consisting of two peaks close together; Antler Peak (10,200 ft.), occupying an isolated position; Quadrant Mountain (10,200 ft.), which slopes to the right; Little Quadrant Mountain (9,800 ft.), of similar shape but farther away; and the majestic 11,155 foot Electric Peak which dominates the skyline.

Of the small furred animals in the park there are otter, mink, weasel, marten, skunk, badger, and the muskrat. The **otter,** being fond of water and living chiefly on fish, makes its home usually under the roots of a large tree overhanging the banks of a s t r e a m. It has webbed hind feet and a thick round tail for use in swimming. The fur of the otter is very fine and of a dark brown color. The **mink** haunts the margins of streams and rivers but is less aquatic than the otter. It preys on small animals and fish, when it can procure them, but lives chiefly on birds; it is smaller than the otter and its fur is yellowish or dark brown. The **common weasel,** or ermine, is a small long-bodied animal with short legs, being the smallest

A FAMILY OF RARE TRUMPETER SWANS
Cob (male), Pen (female) and Cygnets (young).

member of the marten family. It kills grouse, ducks, rabbits and other animals (some ten times its own size) which fact places it in the class of the vicious animals. In summer its coat is brown, but white in winter, a striking manifestation of nature's plan of protection. The marten lives on s m a l l rodents, birds and eggs, and spends so much time in the trees that it is often called the pine marten. Its habitat is on rugged and rocky, forest-covered mountains, seldom in open country. The muskrat, brown furred and aquatic, lives in huts of rushes and mud, or in holes in banks. It is as small as a rat, and has webbed hind feet and a flattened scaly tail. The badger has a broad flat back and like the weasel has very short legs and is very savage. It may be distinguished from the marmot at a distance by its black and white striped face. It lives in burrows and feeds on squirrels and other rodents of every description.

The marmot (woodchuck or ground hog) is a rodent with a squirrel-like face and long incisors for gnawing. He is much larger than any squirrel and is of a rich brown color and is often seen by the roadside sunning himself near his burrow. In autumn he does not store up a winter's supply of provisions like the squirrel but takes on a quantity of fat under the skin, then goes quietly to sleep in his burrow for four or five months when the winter is most severe, hibernating like the bear.

Along the park roads the pine squirrel is often seen, while the chipmunk is likewise abundant.

The picket-pin ground squirrel (Kennicott spermophile) lives in the open country in places like Swan Lake Flat and is seldom seen in rocky or wooded areas. This species hibernates even longer than the marmot, while the other squirrels hibernate little or not at all.

5.80   15.00   Beyond Swan Lake, a favorite nesting place of the rare trumpeter swans, is seen the tip of Bannock Peak (10,400 ft.) at the left edge and beyond Quadrant Mountain. On the opposite side of the road in the distance are seen three peaks of the Washburn Range: (left to right) Prospect Peak (9,300 ft.), Folsom Peak (9,200 ft.), and Cook Peak (9,500 ft.).

The **dogtooth violet** (Erythronium) is found throughout the park in the open woods, near the streams and in the rich wet soil in the vicinity of Swan Lake. The bright yellow flower, about two inches in diameter, rises on a slender stem from between two broad leaves, blossoming early and disappearing before mid-July. It properly belongs to the lily family and is not a violet at all.

6.80   14.00 The south end of Swan Lake Flat.

7.30   13.50 Glacial drift is seen on both sides of the road.

7.40   13.40 At the west is Antler Peak (10,200 ft.).

The **shooting star** (Dodacatheon), one of the most beautiful and interesting of the early flowers, grows in moist, rocky places along the roads and in the open woods and prairies in the park. It blooms during the months of June and July, and in color it is a purplish pink, sometimes white, and it seems appropriately named as the flowers nod with petals bent backward as if they were darting through the air. It is also called the American cowslip.

Coyotes, which are numerous in the lower elevations of the park, like the mountain lion, often prey upon the young and infirm of other species. Washouts and holes in the sides of ravines are used as dens by these wild dogs. They multiply with comparative rapidity; the mating season is in February; pups, usually in litters of from 3 to 10, are born in April. The adult dog averages 25 to 30 pounds in weight, and the length of its head and body is about 3 feet in addition to a bushy tail 12 to 15 inches long. The wild dog, known also as "prairie wolf" or "brush wolf," common to the northwest states, is noted for its cunning and stealth and is useful as a check upon destructive rodents. The startling, hair-raising barking and howling of these animals is frequently heard at night.

Timber wolves, wary and very scarce in the park, are rarely seen.

7.70   13.10 The inconspicuous side road leading west is a service road leading to the water supply aqueduct. No fishing is permitted nearby in the streams flowing from the west toward the road.

8.10   12.70 Side road leads to the south end of Sheepeater Cliffs, a favorite camp site used by the late Howard Eaton, for whom the Howard Eaton Trail in the park was named. From here the Sheepeater Cliffs extend down the Gardner River to the Mammoth-Tower Fall Road and Lava Creek, and eastward up Lava Creek to Undine Falls. This area was inhabited by the nomadic Sheepeater Indians, "whose ancient, but recently deserted, s e c l u d e d

BULL MOOSE—MONARCH OF THE
BUSHY WATERCOURSES

haunts", were discovered by Supt. (1877-1882) Norris. The nearby cliff composed of volcanic rock known as basalt, usually cracks in the form of pentagonal or hexagonal columns. This basalt is of comparatively recent origin and may be seen in Sheepeater Canyon of Gardner River east of Bunsen Peak, in the Grand Canyon of the Yellowstone River near Tower Fall, and at several other places along the road between Tower Fall and the Gallatin Range.

8.20   12.60 Gardner River crossing. The south tributary traversing Willow Park is Obsidian Creek which the road parallels for 3.6 miles. The Gardner River which rises near the south slope of Electric Peak, ten miles away, has three tributaries rising in the Gallatin Range: Fawn, Panther and Indian creeks.

8.60   12.20 Indian Creek Campground is at west across

Obsidian Creek. Western tributaries of Obsidian Creek are Straight and Winter creeks.

10.00   10.80 Parking area. Look for moose. Note old beaver hut near Obsidian Creek.

10.20   10.60 Parking area. Look for moose.

The moose is one of the few big wild animals that is steadily increasing. Moose are abundant about Yellowstone Lake, the upper Yellowstone River near the south boundary of the park, and from Swan Lake Flat to Norris Geyser Basin. They are occasionally seen on the lower slopes of Mt. Washburn, between Grand Canyon and Tower Fall. There are about six hundred in the park. This is the Shiras moose which is black to rusty-brown with light-colored legs. The adult bull averages nine hundred pounds in weight. The mating season is in September; calves are born in May and June. Very rarely there are triplets, occasionally twins, but usually only one calf. Moose antlers, borne only by the bulls, attain full growth in July and are shed in December or January each year.

10.80   10.00 Parking area at Beaver Exhibit. The distant mountains are Trilobite Point (9,900 ft.), Mt. Holmes (10,300 ft.) on which is the Fire Lookout, and Dome Mountain (9,900 ft.). Nearby is a typical beaver dam, of which there are hundreds in the streams of the park.

The beaver is celebrated for

A BEAVER POSES FOR HIS PICTURE

its engineering skill in building dams, some of great extent. For the purpose of providing in the streams a safe refuge from its enemies, it constructs a water entrance to its house and a place below the freezing line for its winter supply of food. The beaver is easily recognized by its broad hairless tail which it uses in swimming. Beavers fell trees which are as much or more than a foot in diameter, by gnawing, and it is said that they cut them so that they will fall toward their pond. The bark of the aspen in the park is highly prized by them as a food. Beavers are seldom seen in the daytime, or in fact at any other time; they work in the evening, beginning about an hour before sundown. The adult beaver is about forty-four inches long, including its tail, which is twelve to fifteen inches in length and four to five inches wide. It weighs forty to fifty pounds and is the largest gnawing animal in North Amer-

ica. It builds two types of dwellings, a hut of sticks or a burrow, also with an underwater entrance in the bank of the stream.

Ground Phlox (Phlox) occur in a green mat on the ground almost covered with a mass of white flowers, at many places along the roads, its habitat being in dry, rocky and sandy soil. Some of the several species in the park have pink or blue flowers.

Harebell (campanula) is a small blue, and sometimes white, bell-shaped flower, which adorns the tip of a very slender stem. It occurs in moist, rocky places along the roads and is quite common in the park in the uplands, blooming from June until September. The name "campanula" is a diminutive of the Italian "campana" meaning bell.

11.40   9.40   A stop is usually made here to sample the sparkling water of **Apollinaris Spring.** (Rest rooms are near by. No camping here.) The

BEAVER HUT IN WINTER

OBSIDIAN CLIFF—VOLCANIC GLASS

principal chemical ingredients of this spring are calcium bicarbonate, silica, magnesium and sodium bicarbonates, sodium sulphate, and potassium chloride, the largest amount of any consisting of about ninety-seven parts per million parts of water by weight. The elevation at the concrete post is 7,337 feet.

11.50	9.30	Obsidian Creek
11.70	9.10	South end of Willow Park.
11.90	8.90	**Lilypad Lake.**
12.20	8.60	**Crystal Spring**

(cold) below the east edge of the road is good drinking water.

North end, **Obsidian Canyon.**

| 12.70 | 8.10 | Parking area. |

The cold spring in the west bank is good drinking water.

12.80   8.00 **Obsidian Cliff Exhibit.** South end of Obsidian Canyon. Beyond Obsidian Creek is **Obsidian Cliff,** described in the exhibit. (See both sides of the exhibit.) The black natural volcanic glass found here was used by the Indians for centuries in making their arrowheads, spearheads, hide-scraping knives, and other implements. On top of this cliff are many obsidian chips marking places where the Indians worked the obsidian. This is the principal outcropping of obsidian in the park although it is found in place in many other areas and mixed in with glacial drift which has been transported several miles. In chemical character this natural glass is the same as the stony rhyolite, common to the entire region.

The **black bear** of the region occurs in two color phases, jet black and dark brown (occasionally one is a very light brown) and cubs of both colors are common in one litter. The average weight of the adult boar, which is 5 to 5½ feet in length, is 250 pounds; the mating season is in June; cubs, usually two but occasionally 1, 3, or 4, are born in January while the sow is still in hibernation, and a cub at birth weighs only 9 to 12 ounces.

In its habits as to food and hibernation, the black bear is similar to the grizzly, and like the latter it is powerful and timid, and when alarmed, or when sow and cubs become separated no wild animal is more dangerous than the fascinating, apparently friendly bear.

Unlike the grizzly, the black bear climbs trees with the agility of a cat, although its claws are short, and it often sleeps on slender limbs that barely support it. The black bear has low shoulders, in contrast to the grizzly, and toward the end of the summer shows a tendency to roly-poly fatness.

There are about 450 black bears in the park according to the most recent count.

(FOR THE PROTECTION OF VISITORS, FEEDING BEARS IN THE PARK IS PROHIBITED.)

13.30   7.50 **Beaver Lake** extends along the road 0.3 of a mile. Across it a beaver dam about a thousand feet in length has been constructed, which is probably the longest beaver dam in the park.

13.70   7.10 Cross unnamed creek. East of the road about 150 yards is a solfataric area where sulphur is being deposited around the sulphurous vents. (Geologists define a solfatara as a fumarole or gas vent which deposits sulphur.)

14.00   6.80 **L e m o n a d e Creek** crossing. One mile up this stream to the east is a large hot spring and solfataric area known as **Amphitheater Springs**, a short distance south of the Lake of the Woods trail. This trail leads to Norris Campground, about seven miles to the southeast. In this Amphitheater Springs area are large amounts of vermilion such as the Indians used for paint.

15.80   5.00 At the west of the road is a group of hot springs and fumaroles known as **Clearwater Springs**. In the water of Obsidian Creek for half a mile along the stream is seen the bright green algae.

15.90   4.90 Near the road are stratified stream and lake deposits of sand and gravel.

16.00   4.80 **Semi-Centennial Geyser.** On the fiftieth anniversary (1922) of the establishment of the park, this great geyser broke out with a furious e x p l o s i o n on August 14. Scalding water carrying mud and rocks washed out the road and killed trees in an area several hundred feet across. The first eruption was estimated to be 300 feet high. The few other discharges were smaller and occurred at increasing intervals until by the end of the season activity ceased. The crater is now a quiescent but somewhat larger hot pool than it was prior to the period of activity. Obsidian Creek flowing through it probably reduces the water temperature sufficiently to prevent further eruptions. This was the most northerly geyser in the park, being about three miles south of Obsidian Cliff and nearly half a mile north of Roaring Mountain; and was named in 1922 by Horace M. Albright then park superintendent (1919-1929).

16.20   4.60 Headwaters of Obsidian Creek at the south edge of the Gardner River drainage are on the slopes at the west. Drainage into the Gibbon and Madison rivers begins at Twin Lakes, one-half mile further south.

16.30   4.50 East of the road is **Roaring Mountain,** with its ashen, furrowed sides and hundreds of steam vents. Although active for many years, it became unusually prominent in 1902—one of its vents producing a loud roar which continued until the orifice became enlarged—and though silent now, the total amount of thermal activity which has been g r a d u a l l y spreading, seems undiminished. The elevation of the concrete post by the road is 7,575 feet and the top of Roaring Mtn. is 8,000 feet. Between the road and the base of the mountain is a body of yellow-green water called **Lemonade Lake.**

ROARING MOUNTAIN AND
LEMONADE LAKE

16.70   4.10 **Twin Lakes.** (North end of northern one). These lakes drain southward into the Gibbon River, which rises north of the Grand Canyon and joins the Firehole River at Madison Junction to form the Madison River.

17.00   3.80 Pond between the Twin Lakes.

17.40   3.40 Twin Lakes (South end of southern one).

17.90   2.90 **Bijah Spring** (hot) is west of the road. An unnamed hot area 1.25 miles southwest of this spring was discovered in 1937 by Curtis Skinner, Asst. Chief Ranger.

18.50   2.30 East of the road is a group of fumaroles.

18.60   2.20 **Nymph Lake** west of the road is in the Gibbon River drainage. **Roadside Springs** between the lake and the road, are hot springs varying in size and character.

18.70   2.10 **Frying Pan Springs** are on both sides of the road. This type of hot spring is common in the Yellowstone region; the frying is caused by innumerable gas vents submerged in shallow water. The elevation 150 feet south of the springs is 7,520 feet.

19.00   1.80 Unnamed creek crossing and unnamed lake.

19.50   1.30 West of the road is a small thermal area.

19.70   1.10 In the distance south of the road is seen Norris Geyser Basin.

20.40   0.40 Side road to **Norris Campground** and **ranger station.**

20.50   0.30 Gibbon River crossing.

20.80   0.00 Norris Junction. **Service road,** east 10.9 miles to Canyon Junction; speed restricted entire distance. Norris Geyser Basin is on The Grand Loop Road just south of Norris Junction.

0.00   14.00 **Norris Junction,** elevation 7,484 ft.

NORRIS GEYSER BASIN

0.30   13.70 North edge of Norris Geyser Basin. At the west of the road along the foot of **Porcelain Terrace** in **Porcelain Basin** are several minor thermal features including Grindstone Springs, Opal Springs, Iris Spring, Onyx Spring, Apple Green Geyser, Blue Geyser and Growler-Spring.

0.40   13.60 **Nuphar Lake** is southeast of the road.

0.50   13.50 **Congress Pool** next to road, usually a boiling muddy pool, sometimes a steam vent, or is quiescent.

Locomotive Spring, on the same side of road (east) and about 100 feet distant, is near the site of a **drill hole** from which at a depth of 265 feet, steam escaped at a pressure of 300 lbs. per square inch, and a temperature of 205° Centigrade *(Hot Springs of the Yellowstone National Park,* Allen and Day, 1935).

0.60   13.40 **Norris Museum** (parking area a short distance behind the museum) contains many interesting exhibits, principally geological, pertaining to this area. The elevation of the

NORRIS GEYSER BASIN

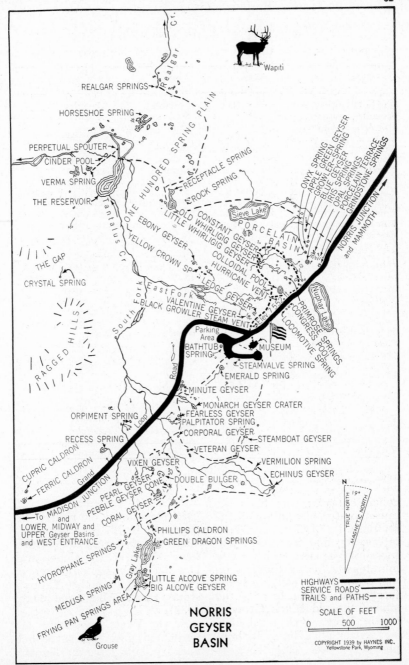

REALGAR SPRINGS
HORSESHOE SPRING
PERPETUAL SPOUTER
CINDER POOL
VERMA SPRING
THE RESERVOIR
Realgar Cr.
Wapiti
ONYX SPRING
APPLE GREEN GEYSER
GROWLER SPRING
BLUE GEYSER
IRIS SPRING
OPAL SPRINGS
PORCELAIN TERRACE
GRINDSTONE SPRINGS
NORRIS JUNCTION and MAMMOTH
RECEPTACLE SPRING
ROCK SPRING
ONE HUNDRED SPRING PLAIN
Sieve Lake
PORCELAIN BASIN
THE GAP
CRYSTAL SPRING
Tantalus Cr.
OLD CONSTANT GEYSER
LITTLE WHIRLIGIG GEYSER
WHIRLIGIG GEYSER
EBONY GEYSER
YELLOW CROWN SP.
COLLOIDAL POOL
HURRICANE VENT
LEDGE GEYSER
East Fork
VALENTINE GEYSER
BLACK GROWLER STEAM VENT
South Fork
RAGGED HILLS
Nuphar Lake
PRIMROSE SPRINGS
CONGRESS POOL
LOCOMOTIVE SPRING
Parking Area
BATHTUB SPRING
MUSEUM
STEAMVALVE SPRING
EMERALD SPRING
MINUTE GEYSER
MONARCH GEYSER CRATER
ORPIMENT SPRING
FEARLESS GEYSER
PALPITATOR SPRING
CORPORAL GEYSER
STEAMBOAT GEYSER
RECESS SPRING
VETERAN GEYSER
VIXEN GEYSER
VERMILION SPRING
ECHINUS GEYSER
CUPRIC CALDRON
FERRIC CALDRON
Grand
Loop
Road
DOUBLE BULGER
PEARL GEYSER
PEBBLE GEYSER CONE
CORAL GEYSER
→ To MADISON JUNCTION and
LOWER, MIDWAY and
UPPER Geyser Basins
and WEST ENTRANCE
PHILLIPS CALDRON
GREEN DRAGON SPRINGS
HYDROPHANE SPRINGS
Gray Lakes
LITTLE ALCOVE SPRING
BIG ALCOVE GEYSER
MEDUSA SPRING
FRYING PAN SPRINGS AREA
Grouse

N
19°
TRUE NORTH
MAGNETIC NORTH

HIGHWAYS
SERVICE ROADS
TRAILS and PATHS

SCALE OF FEET
0   500   1000

NORRIS GEYSER BASIN

GEYSERS AT NORRIS GEYSER BASIN
Geysers dormant at time of this revision are included for record.

Name	Height	Duration	Interval
Apple Green Geyser ...	Few feet....	Variable	Irregular
Arsenic Geyser	6 feet....	20 seconds..	Irregular
Big Alcove Geyser	10-15 ft.....	Almost steady..	None
Blue Geyser	15 feet....	Variable	Irregular
Congress Pool	Few feet....	Variable	Seldom
Constant Geyser	25 feet....	5-30 seconds..	(Dormant)
Coral Geyser	Few feet....	Variable	Irregular
Corporal Geyser	Few feet....	Variable	Irregular
Ebony Geyser	25-50 ft.....	3.5 minutes..	8 hrs. to 2 days
Echinus Geyser	15-30 ft.....	3 minutes..	Seldom
Emerald Spring	20-30 ft.....	Variable	Seldom
Fan Geyser	25 feet....	8-10 minutes..	7 to 19 hours
Fearless Geyser	Few feet....	Variable	Several per day
Harding Geyser	25 feet....	Variable	(Dormant)
Ledge Geyser	60-75 ft.....	Variable	Several per day
Little Whirligig Geyser.	10-20 ft.....	10-20 seconds..	Every few seconds
Minute Geyser	15-20 ft.....	15-30 seconds*.	1 to 3 minutes**
Monarch Geyser	100-200 ft....	6-20 minutes..	(Dormant)
Mud Geyser	8-60 ft.....	5 minutes..	20 minutes
Pearl Geyser	Few feet....	Variable	Irregular
Pebble Geyser	50 feet....	Few minutes..	(Long dormant)
Perpetual Spouter	4 feet....	Steady	None
Steamboat Geyser	25-30 ft.....	1-4 minutes..	2 to 5 minutes
Unnamed Geyser, 100 ft. nw. of Valentine Geys.	20-35 ft.....	Variable	Several per hour
Unnamed Geyser n. of Colloidal Pool	15 feet....	Variable	Several per day
Unnamed Geys., by path n. of Little Whirligig.	3-10 ft.....	Few seconds..	30 to 90 minutes
Valentine Geyser	60-75 ft.....	1.5-2 hours....	18 hrs. to 3 days
Veteran Geyser	1 foot....	Variable	Irregular
Vixen Geyser	18-30 ft.....	20 sec.-5 min...	Irregular
Whirligig Geyser	15-29 ft.....	10 sec.-2 min...	(Dormant)

* Some eruptions last 10 minutes, or more.
** Sometimes inactive for long periods.

concrete post across from the museum at the beginning of the footpath is 7,552 feet. Many interesting and important features may be seen within a few minutes by taking the trip on foot around the short, hard-surfaced path. The first is the site of the old **Black Growler Steam Vent** which until 1928 was extremely active. Its temperature was 284 degrees Fahrenheit—a superheat (at this elevation) of nearly 90 degrees. In 1928 the steam issued mostly from an orifice lower down on the slope—and at a slightly lower temperature. (Hot Springs of the Yellowstone Park, Allen and Day, 1935).

Steam Vents, especially superheated ones, on some hot and dry days, have an element of danger when the gases are invisible—as they sometimes are—instead of the usual steam clouds one can see. On the opposite side of the path, in an alcove, is **Valentine Geyser** which broke out in 1902. It erupts to a height of 60 to 75 feet for 1½ to 2 hours at intervals varying from 18 hours to 3 days. Nearer the path on the same side is **Ledge Geyser** which erupts at an angle, 60 to 75 feet high, several times each day; its duration is variable. On the right side of the path, a few hundred feet further is **Little Whirligig Geyser** near the crater of old Whirligig Geyser (dormant) and Constant Geyser (dormant). It erupts every few seconds to a height of 10 to 20 feet. Seen from the path are a large number of varicolored clear and muddy hot pools of striking beauty and an **Unnamed Geyser**, which plays 15 feet high several times each day. Nearby are **Primrose Springs** and on the opposite side of the path the awesome **Hurricane Vent.** Near the junction of the two forks of the path and between them is a large hot spring called **Colloidal Pool.** Its water contains large quantities of finely divided kaolin and silica which seem to be constantly in suspension.

Trail routes indicated on the accompanying map have been as yet only partly developed. Trails starting back of the museum lead to **Emerald Spring, Steamvalve Spring, Steamboat Geyser,** which erupts 25 to 30 feet in height every 2 to 5 minutes, **Vermilion Spring** and **Echinus Geyser,** which seldom plays; some eruptions attain a height of 30 feet and last three minutes. From here the trail leads northwest past **Veteran** and **Corporal geysers,** both irregular and inconspicuous, thence to **Palpitator Spring** and **Fearless Geyser,** which erupts only a few feet high several times each day. Nearby is the large alcove of Monarch Geyser crater, which when active was the largest geyser in Norris Geyser Basin. It erupted from 100 to 200 feet in height but ceased in 1913. From here the trail leads to **Minute Geyser,** which plays 15 to 20 feet in height for 15 to 30 seconds every 1 to 3 minutes. This geyser in the fall of the year, when ground-waters are usually less abundant, is sometimes inactive for long periods, but when active has been known to erupt constantly for thirty minutes to a maximum period of 3 days. From this geyser near the road the trail leads to the parking area past **Emerald Spring.** This spring has been known to erupt 20 to 30 feet in height.

0.90   13.10 **Minute Geyser** is east of the road.

0.95   13.05 **Tantalus Creek** crossing. This creek, a tributary of Gibbon River, drains the area to the east and south in which are several thermal features in what is known as the **Gray Lakes** area. These are **Phillips Caldron, Green Dragon Springs, Little Alcove Spring, Big Alcove Geyser,** which plays 10 to 15 feet in height almost all of the time,

Medusa Spring, **Hydrophane Springs, Coral Geyser**, which erupts only a few feet at irregular intervals, **Pearl Geyser** also irregular and inconspicuous, and **Vixen Geyser** which is irregular but plays from 18 to 30 feet high several times per day, eruptions lasting from 20 seconds to 5 minutes.

1.10   12.90 West of the road is **Recess Spring**, a quiescent, hot lake.

1.45   12.55 **Ferric Caldron** and **Cupric Caldron** are a few rods north of the road. Ferric Caldron is a small but beautiful cave-type hot spring deriving its coloring from iron oxide but Cupric Caldron has a green algal deposit which accounts for its name, although copper-bearing minerals are not present.

1.60   12.40 Near the road on the east side is a large unnamed hot lake, at the north edge of **Elk Park**, which area is drained by the Gibbon River. This is the south edge of Norris Geyser Basin.

NORRIS GEYSER BASIN
to
MADISON JUNCTION

1.80   12.20 The rounded summit of Mt. Holmes (10,300 ft.) upon which the fire lookout is visible, in the Gallatin Range, is seen in the northwest.

2.40   11.60 South end of **Elk Park**. Many wapiti (American elk) are frequently seen in this meadow. Look also for wild ducks, Canadian geese, blue herons and other wild life both here and in **Gibbon Mead**ows, which the road traverses south of Elk Park.

The **wapiti** (elk), of which there are about 10,650 head in the park are widely distributed. This majestic animal is as tall as a horse, handsomely formed, and has a luxurious dark mane. The bull is armed with imposing antlers which attain full growth in September and are shed during the months of February and March. It seems remarkable that antlers of such great size can be grown to maturity in a few months, to be lost and regrown each year. In summer the wapiti is reddish-brown, but in winter the bull is pale gray-brown and the cow brown. The average weight of an adult bull is 700 pounds; the mating season is September and October; calves, usually one and sometimes twins, are born in May and June. This is a stately species; "even the young step about with the air of a gamecock."

2.75   11.25 From here to Madison Junction (11.25 miles to the southwest) the road follows the Gibbon River. **Gibbon River Rapids** are just west of this point.

2.85   11.15 Downstream from the small parking area is **Duck Rock** in Gibbon River. It has a stream-eroded pedestal and looks something like a huge duck head.

3.00   11.00 **Chocolate Pots** are on both sides of the stream. There is also a small spouter submerged in the river not far from the near shore.

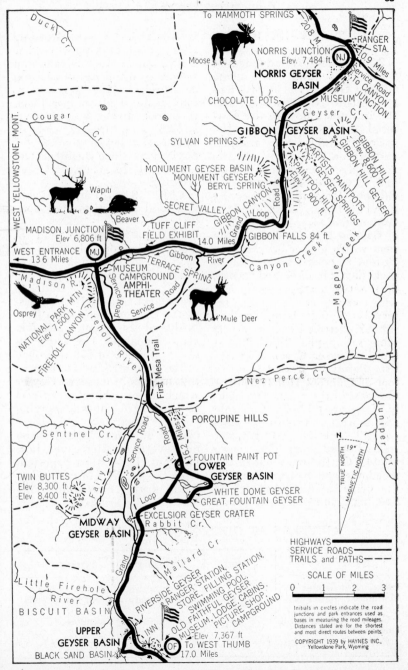

To MAMMOTH SPRINGS

Duck Cr.

208 M.

RANGER STA.

NORRIS JUNCTION
Elev. 7,484 ft

109 Miles

Moose

Service Road

To CANYON JUNCTION

NORRIS GEYSER BASIN

CHOCOLATE POTS

MUSEUM

Cougar Cr.

Geyser Cr.

GIBBON GEYSER BASIN

SYLVAN SPRINGS

Elev. 8,600 ft
GIBBON HILL

GIBBON HILL GEYSER

MONUMENT GEYSER BASIN
MONUMENT GEYSER
BERYL SPRING

ARTISTS PAINTPOTS
GEYSER SPRINGS

PAINTPOT HILL
Elev. 7,900 ft.

WEST YELLOWSTONE, MONT.

Wapiti

SECRET VALLEY

GIBBON CANYON

Loop

Grand

Road

Beaver

TUFF CLIFF
FIELD EXHIBIT

14.0 Miles

GIBBON FALLS 84 ft.

MADISON JUNCTION
Elev. 6,806 ft

MJ

WEST ENTRANCE
← 13.6 Miles

Gibbon River

Canyon Creek

Magpie Creek

Madison R.

Osprey

NATIONAL PARK MTN.
Elev. 7,500 ft

FIREHOLE CANYON

TERRACE SPRING

MUSEUM
CAMPGROUND
AMPHI-THEATER

Service Road

Service Road

Firehole River

Mule Deer

First Mesa Trail

Nez Perce Cr.

Juniper Cr.

Sentinel Cr.

Service Road

16.2 Miles

Road

PORCUPINE HILLS

FOUNTAIN PAINT POT

LOWER GEYSER BASIN

TWIN BUTTES
Elev. 8,300 ft
Elev. 8,400 ft

Fairy Cr.

Loop

WHITE DOME GEYSER
GREAT FOUNTAIN GEYSER

EXCELSIOR GEYSER CRATER

MIDWAY GEYSER BASIN

Rabbit Cr.

Grand

Mallard Cr.

Little Firehole River

BISCUIT BASIN

UPPER GEYSER BASIN

BLACK SAND BASIN

INN

RIVERSIDE GEYSER
RANGER STATION,
STORE, FILLING STATION,
SWIMMING POOL,
MUSEUM, LODGE, CABINS,
PICTURE SHOP,
CAMPGROUND
OLD FAITHFUL GEYSER

OF

Elev. 7,367 ft
To WEST THUMB
17.0 Miles

N
TRUE NORTH
MAGNETIC NORTH
19°

HIGHWAYS ━━━
SERVICE ROADS ━━━
TRAILS and PATHS ─ ─ ─

SCALE OF MILES

0   1   2   3

Initials in circles indicate the road
junctions and park entrances used as
bases in measuring the road mileages.
Distances stated are for the shortest
and most direct routes between points.

GIBBON GEYSER BASIN

3.50　10.50　North edge of Gibbon Meadows. The name **Gibbon Geyser Basin**, originally given to Norris Geyser Basin, is applied now to the scattered groups of geysers, hot springs, and other thermal phenomena beginning at the north edge of Gibbon Meadows and extending southward into Gibbon Canyon as far as the Beryl Spring area. Included are **Gibbon Hill Geyser** at the foot of **Gibbon Hill** (8,600 ft.) to the east, which geyser erupts 15 to 25 feet in height several times each day, an unnamed geyser in the Geyser Springs group, which erupts at six minute intervals 25 feet high, another similar unnamed geyser in this same group near the headwaters of Geyser Creek, and **Artists Paintpots** near the north foot of **Paintpot Hill** (7,900 ft.) also east of the road. The newly discovered (1938) fumarole area is west and south of Paintpot Hill. It is here that natural, steam-heated bear dens were found. On the west side of the meadows are **Sylvan Springs**, the principal one of which is **Evening Primrose Spring** which is similar in size to Morning Glory Pool at Upper Geyser Basin, but in color is cadmium yellow with touches of crimson at the edges. Nearby is a roaring steam vent and a black mud pot and the ground is strewn with quartz crystals which are relics of rhyolite porphyry long since disintegrated.

3.90　10.10　Geyser Creek crossing.

4.20　9.80　Parking area and trail to **Artists Paintpots**, 0.5 mile.

4.50　9.50　North end of Gibbon Canyon, elevation 7,336 feet, at the south edge of Gibbon Meadows.

4.60　9.40　The trail to **Monument Geyser Basin** crosses the Gibbon River on a footbridge at this point. The trip requiring about 1½ hours includes a climb of 650 feet. One of the most striking features of this area is **Monument Geyser** which erupts almost steadily 4 to 9 feet high. It is a spraying geyser having a cylindrical cone 6 or 8 feet high. Nearby are several smaller cones, now dormant. The silica deposited from the spray is in part gelatinous, drying to a white powder. In this group are a large

GEYSERS AT GIBBON GEYSER BASIN

NAME	HEIGHT	DURATION	INTERVAL
Gibbon Hill Geyser	15–25 ft.....	Few minutes..	Several per day
Monument Geyser	4– 9 ft.....	Almost steady .	Every few seconds
Unnamed Geyser in Geyser Springs group	25 feet....	Few minutes..	6 minutes
Unnamed Geyser in Geyser Springs group	Few feet....	Variable	Undetermined

MONUMENT GEYSER—MONUMENT GEYSER BASIN

boiling sulphur caldron and a superheated steam vent, and many other smaller springs some of which deposit salts of arsenic, (realgar and orpiment). This thermal area was discovered in 1878 by P. W. Norris, then superintendent.

5.00   9.00 Gibbon River crossing. The thermal area east of the road and river is at the foot of the cliff, behind which is the newly discovered fumarole area previously referred to.

5.35   8.65 **Beryl Spring**, 20 feet in diameter, at the west of the road, churns constantly and overflows copiously. It is one of the hottest springs in the region. Behind it in the bank, is a superheated steam vent which is always active.

5.45   8.55 In the gulch a few rods up the side of the slope is a paintpot and hot spring area, considered a southerly continuation of Monument Geyser Basin, which area marks the south edge of Gibbon Geyser Basin.

5.85   8.15 The high cliff south of this point shows flow structure in the rhyolite porphyry. The lavender coloring, characteristic of Gibbon Canyon may be due to the predominance of orthoclase, a pink feldspar in the rhyolite porphyry.

6.20   7.80 Gibbon River crossing.

6.80   7.20 C o n t i n u i n g southward from the main road is the first mesa trail, originally the Norris Road, built in 1878.

7.20   6.80 Gibbon River crossing.

7.45   6.55 In the bank at the side of the road is a group of cold springs.

8.30   5.70 **Iron Spring** (cold) at the east edge of the road. The waters of this spring contain small amounts of silica, sodium bicarbonate, sodium sulphate, ferric oxide and other salts in lesser quantities. There is no prohibition against drinking this water.

8.45   5.55   The bank above the road shows a cross section of glacial lake sediment. **Secret Valley,** at the west, widens out above the road and is a fine grazing area for wild animals. **Secret Valley Creek** crossing.

8.55   5.45   A cliff of fairly fresh rhyolite porphyry rises above the road.

8.80   5.20   Parking area at **Gibbon Falls.** These falls are 84 feet high and are beautiful both at high and low water.

8.95   5.05   Parking area from which Gibbon Falls may be seen. In the bank above the road is a fine example of glacial drift.

9.70   4.30   Second Mesa Road Junction. **Service Road,** south 5.65 miles to Grand Loop Road near Cascades of the Firehole River. Road is narrow, crooked and slow.

13.00   1.00   **Terrace Spring** is a large hot lake just beyond the turn in the road. Its waters flow under the road and spread out on the terraces nearby.

13.05   0.95   The terraces of Terrace Spring derive their coloring from algae, a low form of plant life, which in this instance is rather leathery in texture and is of two predominating colors, green and Indian red.

Lupine (Lupinus) is a purplish blue flower which is sometimes called a wild pea. Some of the rare white flowers of this species have been found in the park. The name is derived from "lupus," a wolf, because its roots were once thought to devour the fertility of the soil. Lupines, of which there are several species in the park, bloom from June until September and stand from 1 to 3 feet high. The seeds were used as food by the Indians.

14.00   0.00   **Madison Junction.** The road leading to West Entrance (13.6 miles), follows down the Madison River.

NATIONAL PARK MOUNTAIN NEAR MADISON JUNCTION

WEST ENTRANCE

West Yellowstone, Montana, just outside the western boundary of the park, came into existence about 1907 when the railroad was completed to the park. It is a thriving, typically-Western town which caters principally to the needs of travelers, and both guests and operators of dude ranches and hunting lodges in the vicinity.

A branch line of the **Union Pacific Railroad** serves West Yellowstone where it has erected a large stone depot and nearby a spacious dining room. Buses of the Yellowstone Park Company connect with the railroad at West Yellowstone; service is twice daily during the tourist season. It was the progressive spirit of the first decade of the new century that motivated the building of the Yellowstone Park Line by the Oregon Short Line Railroad Company, now the central operating unit of the integrated Union Pacific Railroad. It was the spirit of Edward Henry Harriman, whose life's work only time can evaluate; of W. H. Bancroft, the vice president and general manager of the O. S. L. R. R. Co., the man who spoke with unconscious humor of "my" engine, "my" station, "my" railroad; of William Ashton, the engineer; of Stradley, the reconnoissance engineer; of Frank Jay Haynes, president of the Monida & Yellowstone Stage Company, who envisioned a tour of Yellowstone Park through the West Entrance in comfort and convenience for the multitudes. The movement for a western entrance by rail was sparked by Mr. Haynes of the Monida & Yellowstone Stage Company, and in 1898 this company made a stage connection with the Oregon Short Line at Monida, 60 miles on a direct line from the west boundary of the park or 75 miles by the stage road. Concerning this condition, particularly the stage route from Monida to Dwelle's Hotel, near the present town of West Yellowstone, Mont., an early survey reported:

"The 69 miles from Monida to Dwelle's Hotel in one day over unworked roads, very rough and stony in places, must be an experience that the most hardy would not care to repeat the same season, and it is considered remarkable that the Monida & Yellowstone Stage Company carried as many passengers as it has."

Following a complete inspection trip in August, 1905, by E. H. Harriman, during which he visited Yellowstone Park with F. J. Haynes, and while he was at Old Faithful, Mr. Harriman authorized construction of the branch line to the West Entrance. Construction work commenced in October, 1905, and the line was opened for traffic between St. Anthony and Marysville, Idaho, 16.4 miles, on June 15, 1906. During 1906 and 1907 track was laid to mile post 56. The principal engineering features were about 6 miles of very heavy work in Warm River Canyon, 23 to 30 miles from St. Anthony, and the crossing of the Continental Divide through Rea's Pass at an elevation of 6,932.3 feet. Transcontinental railroad service was established by the Union Pacific Railroad to the West Entrance of the park during the summer of 1908. In 1898 the **Monida & Yellowstone Stage Company** was organized by Frank Jay Haynes, who secured a franchise from the Department of the Interior to operate stages through the park for guests entering at the West Entrance. This company operated for ten years before the railroad completed its branch line to the boundary. In 1913 the name of the stage company was changed to the **Yellowstone-Western Stage Company** and it operated until 1917 when the transportation in the park was motorized.

Gallatin Gateway, 85 miles north of West Yellowstone, is reached by **The Milwaukee Road** which company completed a rustic arch south of Gallatin Gateway in time for its first service to the park, Aug. 1, 1926. On June 18, 1927, **Gallatin Gateway Inn** (Gallatin G a t e w a y, Montana) was opened. It is served by the buses of the Yellowstone Park Co., which connect with the railroad here.

West of town is the **West Yellowstone Airport,** the highest regularly used air-mail field in the United States.

The **Western Air Lines** offers special trips over the park —a charter tour by air—and a special scenic flight via Jackson Hole and the Teton Mountains including Old Faithful (Upper Geyser Basin) and Lower Geyser Basin.

The West Entrance is the only portal that may be reached by plane direct, using United Airlines to Salt Lake City and thence via Western Air Lines or going via Northwest Airlines to Butte or Helena, Montana, and thence via Western Air Lines to West Yellowstone.

WEST ENTRANCE to MADISON JUNCTION

This entrance road joins The Grand Loop Road of the Park at Madison Junction 13.6 miles to the east. High lights are the beautiful drive through a forest of lodgepole pines and upstream along the Madison R i v e r through Madison Canyon, about 10 miles northeast of Echo Canyon, made famous by the well-known Jim Bridger story, that upon retiring at night he would holler, "Wake up, Jim," and by morning the echo would return just in time to arouse him for the new day. Through West Entrance is one of the earliest

MT. HAYNES, MADISON CANYON

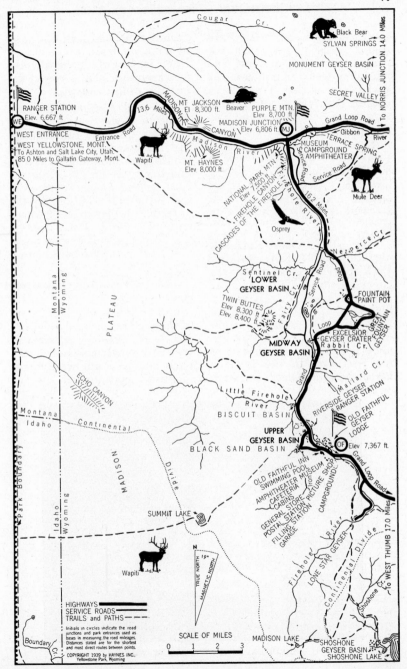

SCALE OF MILES

0   1   2   3

HIGHWAYS ━━━
SERVICE ROADS ────
TRAILS and PATHS ----

Initials in circles indicate the road junctions and park entrances used as bases in measuring the road mileages. Distances stated are for the shortest and most direct routes between points.

COPYRIGHT 1939 by HAYNES INC.
Yellowstone Park, Wyoming

routes in the Yellowstone Park region. The "Beaver Canyon route", northwest of West Yellowstone, was as famous in the early days as the "Trail Creek route", southwest of Livingston, from Fort Ellis to the Yellowstone River.

(NOTE: The first distance figure shown at the beginning of key paragraphs, applies to those traveling in the same direction as the sequence of paragraphs. Those traveling in the opposite direction, read the paragraphs in reverse order and use the second, instead of the first, distance figure.)

0.00   13.60   **West Entrance,** elevation 6,667 feet. **National Park Service** rangers at the checking stations here, as at all park entrances, record all vehicles entering and leaving the park and issue season permits upon payment of the motor vehicle license fees prescribed by the Secretary of the Interior. Firearms are sealed. Dogs are permitted in the park but must be kept on leash or in crates. Upon leaving the park all visitors are requested to report the number of fish caught.

Fish and Fishing. In the Madison River and other waters near the West Entrance are the rainbow and Loch Leven trout, the Montana grayling, and Rocky Mountain whitefish. Fishing licenses are required in the three states adjoining the park, but no license is required within the park. Trails used by the ranger patrols extend north and south along the park boundary.

0.05   13.55   Ranger quarters south of road.

0.10   13.50   On both sides of the road for several miles are stands of lodgepole pines; this tree is the most common in the park and is a tall weedy tree identified by the fact that its

LOCH LEVEN AND RAINBOW TROUT

needles are in pairs. (This area was formerly called Christmas Tree Park but the name had already been applied to the forested area at the headwaters of Winter Creek, 15 miles northeast of this point.)

2.05   11.55   **Montana-Wyoming State Line.** In general this state line parallels the west boundary of the park, the part of the park in Montana being about two miles wide except along the northwest and north boundaries where it is irregular.

4.10   9.50   South of the road is the site of the former Riverside Station. On the opposite side is the Madison River, a tributary of the Missouri River, and in the distance may be seen many mountains of the Gallatin Range (identified in detail in the descriptions of the route from park headquarters at Mammoth Hot Springs to Norris Geyser Basin). Trails used by the ranger patrols lead to the northeast and southeast to The Grand Loop Road.

7.20   6.40   The small bush common in this area is the sagebrush (Artemisia tridentata), a fragrant blue-gray bush common to the western plains.

7.60   6.00   Madison River crossing.

8.50   5.10   West end of **Madison Canyon.**

10.15   3.45   **Mt. Jackson** (8,200 ft.) is north of the road. This was named for William H. Jackson, a member of the Hayden Survey of 1871, who at that time took the first photographs of Yellowstone Park features.

10.60   3.00   **Mt. Haynes** (8,-000 ft.) is south of the road beyond the Madison River. It was named for Frank Jay Haynes (1853-1921) who came to the park for the first time in 1881 and spent 40 years as a concessioner in the park, conducting picture shops and stage lines; he was also the president of the first motor line in the park (1916), known as the Cody-Sylvan Pass Motor Company, which operated from Cody, Wyoming, to Yellowstone Lake.

11.70   1.90   A cold spring suitable for drinking is at the side of the road.

12.90   0.70   East end of Madison Canyon.

13.50   0.10   Directly south of the road is the point of confluence of the Gibbon and Firehole rivers, which at this junction form the Madison River.

13.60   0.00   **Madison Junction,** elevation 6,806 feet.

MADISON JUNCTION
to
UPPER GEYSER BASIN
(OLD FAITHFUL)

0.00   16.20   **Madison Junction** elevation 6,806 feet.

The road up Firehole River to Upper Geyser Basin (Old Faithful), 16.2 miles, runs almost directly south and traverses three important areas—Lower Geyser Basin, Midway Geyser Basin, and Upper Geyser Basin. There are four important side roads: one to Fountain Paint Pot, another to Firehole Lake, White Dome, and

Great Fountain geysers, a side spur to Biscuit Basin, and a loop road to Black Sand Basin, including Emerald Pool and other features at Upper Geyser Basin. Together this group of thermal areas is the most important in the entire world.

Nearby is **Madison Museum** containing exhibits principally of historical interest. Rest rooms and an Amphitheater are in the nearby campground.

Just beyond the junction of the Firehole and Gibbon rivers, which form the Madison River, is **National Park Mountain** (7,-500 ft.) named to commemorate the inception of the national park idea, which occurred on Sept. 19, 1870, in the camp of the Expedition of 1870 at the foot of this mountain opposite the junction of the streams. Cornelius Hedges is credited with having first made the suggestion that the region including the awe-inspiring, curious manifestations of nature, which that expedition had just discovered, should be made a national park and thus be preserved in its natural state for all time.

To the north of this junction is **Purple Mountain** (8,700 ft.), the highest visible promontory.

0.08   16.12   East side road leads to campground and rest rooms.

0.10   16.10   Gibbon River crossing. Side road south of the river is a service road which reenters The Grand Loop Road at the Cascades of the Firehole River.

0.30   15.90   Across the Firehole River is seen the steep face of National Park Mountain (7,-500 ft.).

0.40   15.80   A cold spring at the side of the road is suitable for drinking. North end of **Firehole Canyon.**

0.45   15.75   Osprey nest on rock pinnacle across Firehole River. The osprey or fish hawk is one of the largest and most important birds in this area. It nests in treetops or on rock pinnacles and may be seen at Yellowstone Lake, Grand Canyon, and many other places in the park.

1.10   15.10   **Firehole Falls,** about 40 feet high, may be seen at this point. There is a small parking area and a geological exhibit here that describes the walls of Firehole Canyon.

CASCADES OF THE FIREHOLE RIVER

2.32   13.88   **Cascades of the Firehole River.**

2.35   13.85   Jct. **Service roads,** northwest fork 2.4 miles to Madison Junction, north fork 5.65 miles to Grand Loop Road at point 4.3 miles east of Madison Junction. Service roads, both forks, are narrow, crooked and slow.

2.60   13.60   At the north is seen the 8,700 foot summit of Purple Mountain, 3 miles away.

3.24   12.96   In the large rocks along Firehole River are fine examples of lodgepole pines growing with practically no soil.

4.20   12.00   South end of Firehole Canyon.

Firehole River was named in the very early days, not from the fact that hot springs and geysers adorn its banks for many miles and pour their hot waters into the stream but because the trappers who frequented this region found a burnt-over, heavily forested "hole" or valley through which the river coursed, and from the name "burnt hole" developed the present name of the stream. Jim Bridger is credited with having said that in this marvelous area the water ran downhill so fast that it heated the river bed, which conclusion was borne out by the fact that at some places hot springs in the bed of the river do keep the rock hot under the cold water of the stream. Before bridges were built the trappers forded this stream barefooted, not having waders in their dunnage, and believing that they should keep their boots or mocassins as well as their powder dry, and it was this practice that brought about this one of Jim Bridger's immortal stories.

The water of Firehole River is cold, and inhabited by trout.

Forest fires antedated human occupancy here as in other areas. They are caused often by lightning and occasionally, it is said, by frictional heat developed by tree trunks rubbing together in a heavy windstorm starting a fire in the resinous wood; but human beings, through carelessness, cause most of the forest fires.

5.65   10.55   Jct. **Service road** south 5.1 miles across Nez Perce Cr., and Firehole River, missing the principal attractions of both the Lower and Midway geyser basins, to the Grand Loop Road at a point south of Midway Geyser Basin. Road is narrow, crooked and slow.

6.20   10.00   Nez Perce Creek crossing.

6.50   9.70   **Porcupine Hills,** elevation 7,350 feet, at the east are at the north edge of Lower Geyser Basin. North of these hills is the **Morning Mist Group** of hot springs of minor importance. The **Quagmire Group,** south of the hills has one named feature, **Snort Geyser** (now a steam vent), which is in the slope below **Rock Point—** an eminence of glacial drift cemented with hydrothermal deposits.

LOWER GEYSER BASIN

7.45   8.75   **Twin Buttes** whose summits rise to elevations of 7,900 and 7,800 ft., (southern one is the higher), are at the southwest. Small geysers **Clepsydra** (southern one), and **Kaleidoscope** are frequently seen in action. East of the road is a group of named hot springs and **Thud Geyser**. **Lone Spring** is about 500 yards at the east.

7.90   8.30 North junction of Fountain Paint Pot and parking area road. **Leather Pool** nearby is so named on account of the leathery algal life which lines its basin. **Fountain Paint Pot**, formerly called Mammoth Paint Pot, was renamed to avoid confusion with the Mammoth area. It is a large hot caldron of clay, quartz and opal, blending in color from white to tints of pale orange and pink. Its sound varies from "plop, plop" at normal times to a splashing sound when water is abundant. The most successful photographs of Fountain Paint Pot have been taken about midafternoon, when the light is at an angle.

Silex Spring is southeast of the Fountain Paint Pot; and **Celestine Pool** at the south.

GEYSERS AT LOWER GEYSER BASIN

Geysers dormant at time of this revision are included for record.

NAME	HEIGHT	DURATION	INTERVAL
Bead Geyser	10-15 ft.....	Variable	Irregular
Bellefontaine Geyser ...	Few feet....	Variable	Frequent
Clepsydra Geyser	5-25 ft.....	Few seconds..	3 minutes
Fitful Geyser	3 feet....	Variable	Unrecorded
Fortress Geyser	4- 6 ft....	Few seconds..	Frequent
Fountain Geyser	50-75 ft.....	10-60 minutes..	Seldom*
Gray Bulger Geyser ...	1 foot....	30 seconds..	1 minute
Great Fountain Geyser.	90 feet....	45-75 minutes..	8-15 hours
Jet Geyser	10-15 ft.....	19-30 minutes..	Unrecorded
Kaleidoscope Geyser ...	25-35 ft.....	1½-2 minutes.	8½-10½ minutes
Mound Geyser	Unrecorded .	Unrecorded ...	Unrecorded
Narcissus Geyser	2-16 ft.....	Unrecorded ...	Unrecorded
Pink Cone Geyser	6-17 ft.....	30 min.-1 hr. ..	Seldom
Rosette Geyser	10-15 ft.....	20-50 seconds..	1.5-2.5 minutes
Sand Geyser	Few inches..	Variable	Several per day
Snort Geyser	Unrecorded .	Unrecorded ...	Unrecorded**
Spasm Geyser	2- 3 ft.....	2.5 hours	Unrecorded
Sprinklers Geysers, The.	Few feet....	Unrecorded ...	Unrecorded
Steady Geyser	6 ft.	Steady	None
Thud Geyser	5-8 ft......	Unrecorded ...	Unrecorded
White Dome Geyser ...	18-30 ft.....	1½-2½ min. ..	20-30 minutes
Young Hopeful Geyser .	15-20 ft.....	65-80 seconds..	(Dormant)

*Sometimes inactive for long periods.
**Now a steam vent.

8.00   8.20 South junction of Fountain Paint Pot road.

FIREHOLE LAKE LOOP

8.10   8.10 North end of scenic loop road, 3.3 miles in length. The distances from this junction are given in parentheses the junction being (0.0 mi.). **Hot Lake** (0.9 mi.) at right. This is one of the largest hot lakes in the park. **Steady Geyser** (1.02 mi.) erupts about 6 feet all the time. It is a perpetual spouter t h e r e f o r e, rather than a geyser. **Black Warrior Springs** (1.07 mi.). These hot springs also at the right, supply a large amount of the hot water for Hot Lake. **Firehole Lake** (and creek crossing) (1.12 mi.) at the left is the famous one in which gas bubbles deep down in the water, giving the blue coloring, led early explorers to believe that burning gas was coming out of the orifice. **Young Hopeful Geyser** (1.3 mi.) at the left (now dormant). Creek crossing (1.31 mi.). Tangled Creek crossing (1.45 mi.). **Tank Spring** (1.55 mi.) at the left. **Bead Geyser** (1.65 mi.) at the right, is very irregular but when in action erupts 10 to 15 feet in height. **Pink Cone Geyser** (1.7 mi.) is seldom in eruption. It plays 6 to 17 feet high from 30 minutes to an hour during eruptions. Tangled Creek crossing (2.00 mi.). **White Dome Geyser** (2.08 mi.) has the most conspicuous mound of any geyser in Lower Geyser Basin. Eruptions 18-30 feet high occur two or three

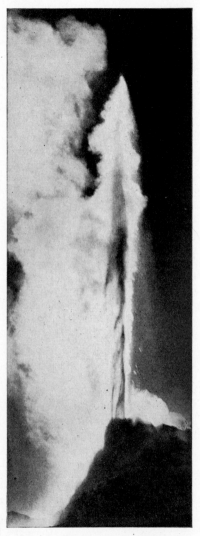

WHITE DOME GEYSER

times each hour. **Great Fountain Geyser** (2.28 mi.). Eruptions occur at intervals of from 8 to 15 hours, lasting from 45 to 75 minutes, and the greatest height attained is 90 feet. **Surprise Pool** (2.42 mi.) at the right of the road is typical of the superheated hot springs in the park which do not boil even though the temperature of the water is higher than the normal boiling point of water at this elevation. **White Creek** crossing (2.47 mi.). **Firehole Spring** (2.52 mi.) is a hot spring at the north of the road which at times exhibits the "fire" appearance caused by escaping gas. **Broken Egg Spring** (2.57 mi.) also at the north of the road is a small circular hot spring with algal coloring thought by some to simulate a "broken egg". South end of scenic loop road (3.3 mi.).

GRAND LOOP ROAD

9.20   7.00   South junction of Firehole Lake Loop and the Grand Loop Road.   Straight road from here north to Fountain Paint Pot crosses **White Creek** (southerly stream) and **Tangled Creek,** both tributaries of Firehole River.

9.30   6.90   Path west 300 yards to unnamed, deep lake some 200 yards across and roughly circular in shape—nesting place for waterfowl and inhabitated by trout.

MIDWAY GEYSER BASIN

10.20   6.00   Parking area at north edge of Midway Geyser Basin and footbridge to several important features including **Excelsior Geyser Crater,** a geyser of great magnitude which played last in the year 1888.   When active it erupted 300 feet high at 1 to 4 hour intervals for periods of from 4 minutes to 1½ hours.   The overflow from this crater measured about 1934 is tremendous —approximately one and one-half billion gallons of scalding water annually (6 cubic feet per second).

Turquoise Pool, large and quiescent, is 100 feet west. Its translucent water, due to minute particles held in suspension, is unique in point of coloring. About 160 feet farther

GEYSERS AT MIDWAY GEYSER BASIN

Geysers dormant at time of this revision are included for record.

NAME	HEIGHT	DURATION	INTERVAL
Catfish Geyser	1 foot....	Constant	None
Excelsior Geyser	200–300 ft....	4 min.–1.5 hrs.	1-4 hours*
Flood Geyser	Few feet....	Unrecorded ...	Unrecorded
Imperial Geyser	100–125 ft....	1- 5 hours ...	12-15 hours*
Spray Geyser	5–20 ft.....	12-38 minutes..	2-31 minutes

* Now dormant.   (Excelsior ceased 1888; Imperial ceased 1929.)

west is **Opal Pool** at the south of which is **Grand Prismatic Spring,** the largest hot spring in the geyser basin. The slopes on all sides of this pool, which is nearly 400 feet across, are beautifully colored and at times the colors of the pool and its border are reflected in the rising steam, which accounts for the name given this feature. Several hundred feet east of Grand Prismatic Spring, is **Indigo Spring,** about 200 feet from the river. A walking tour around the newly constructed path (1938) to the principal features of this geyser basin is well worth while.

Included in Midway Geyser Basin are two interesting areas away from the beaten path. One of these is just south of Twin Buttes which may be seen to the west. In this area are Imperial and Spray geysers. **Imperial Geyser,** when active, erupted 125 feet high every 12 to 15 hours, eruptions lasting 1 to 5 hours. This geyser was first discovered in action on July 10, 1928; it ceased to play in September of the following year. **Spray Geyser** also at the south edge of the south Twin Butte has been active for a great many years. It erupts at intervals of 2 to 31 minutes to a height of 5 to 20 feet, eruptions lasting from 12 to 38 minutes. The other area, which will be mentioned further on, at the south end of Midway Geyser Basin, is drained by Rabbit Creek.

10.30   5.90 On the opposite side of the road is **Bluff Point,** elevation 7,425 feet, which rises about a hundred feet above the road and it may be ascended most conveniently up the slope on the same side as the footbridge. Splendid photographs of the central portion of this geyser basin may be taken from Bluff Point.

10.85   5.35 On the near bank of Firehole River is seen the crater of **Flood Geyser** which erupts only a few feet at irregular intervals.

11.40   4.80 **Catfish Geyser,** a small perpetual spouter, is on the east bank of the river.

11.45   4.75 **Rabbit Creek** crossings. At the headwaters of this creek, a mile or so to the east, is one of the largest and most beautiful blue hot pools in the park. Near it is a paintpot and fumarole area with brilliant colorings, both mineral and algal. For several hundred yards the main fork of this creek is depositing sinter (hydrous silicon dioxide known as geyserite) so that the channel throughout the distance is built up in a fascinating series of natural dikes, canals and terraces which are quite different from those found in any other part of the park. Several tributaries rise in natural wells along the south side of this creek and pour their scalding water into Rabbit Creek. At the south are some large hot pools, and further south, along the foot of the hills, is evidently a fault line, indicated by numerous, mostly inconspicuous hot springs and fissures.

Three species of rabbits, or

more properly hares, are found in the park. The **varying hare or snowshoe rabbit** is the common species found only at elevations below 8,000 feet. In autumn its brown summer coat changes to white and gives it continued protective coloration in the snowy landscapes of winter. A rarer species is the **white-tailed jack rabbit,** which also assumes a white winter coat and is unique among our jack rabbits in this characteristic. It may be distinguished from the snowshoe rabbit by its white tail and longer ears, and it inhabits the lower elevations near the North Entrance and in the vicinity of Mammoth, where the **cottontail** is also found.

11.47   4.73   Near the road on the east side is a group of hot springs and a small geyser, which is unnamed and whose height, interval and duration have not yet been recorded.

11.60   4.60   The service road from the north end of Lower Geyser Basin joins The Grand Loop Road at this point.

11.70   4.50   The group of small hot springs on the opposite side of the Firehole River are at the south edge of Midway Geyser Basin.

13.30   2.90   In the distance (south) is seen a beautiful unnamed fall of considerable height. It is at its best in the spring of the year when the supply of surface water is abundant.

13.90   2.30   North edge of **Upper Geyser Basin.**

Geyser tables in this book include all known geysers of importance, hot springs which erupt only occasionally, perpetual spouters and, for record, a few geysers dormant at the time of this revision—142 of the total of some 200 known geysers in the park. Some geysers have varied only slightly since the park was e s t a b l i s h e d (1872), a few have become dormant or extinct, but enough new ones have broken out to justify the conclusion that total geyseric activity in the park today is neither appreciably greater nor less than it was when its geysers were first discovered.

Obviously in a strong wind a geyser's height will be considerably less than when the air is still. Height, duration and interval may vary considerably during seasonal and cyclical variations in the amount of water available. Some geysers lapse when water is abundant; others when the supply is subnormal. Height applies to the water column and not to the clouds of steam which at times rise several hundred feet. Heights in some cases were measured by triangulation; others are estimated. The tables in this book are the result of a study of a systematic compilation of all available data on each geyser, including observations made during the past season, but since geysers are changing constantly the figures given, while of value as records, may not apply to future activity.

GEYSERS AT UPPER GEYSER BASIN

Geysers dormant at time of this revision are included for record.

NAME	HEIGHT	DURATION	INTERVAL
Anemone Geyser	Few feet....	30 seconds..	Frequent
Artemisia Geyser	15-35 ft.....	10-25 minutes..	24-30 hours
Atomizer Geyser	20 feet....	1 minute....	Once per day
Beach Spring	2 feet....	Varies	2-3 hours
Beehive Geyser	200-219 ft....	2- 8 minutes..	Seldom
Big Cub Geyser	30 feet.....	8 minutes..	(Dormant)
Bijou Geyser	Few feet....	Almost steady .	Very frequent
Black Pearl Geyser ...	Few feet....	Few seconds..	Frequent
Unnamed geyser near The Bottomless Pit...	35 feet....	Unrecorded	(Dormant)
Bulger Spring	3- 7 ft.....	Unrecorded ...	Once per day
Cascade Geyser	30 feet....	Unrecorded ...	(Dormant)
Castle Geyser	65-100 ft....	25-30 minutes..	24-30 hours
Catfish Geyser	8 feet....	Almost steady.	Very frequent
Cauliflower Geyser	Boils up....	Unrecorded ...	12-24 hours
Chimney Cone	Unrecorded..	Unrecorded ...	(Dormant)
Chinaman Spring	40 feet....	2 minutes..	(Dormant)
Churn Geyser	Unrecorded..	Unrecorded ...	Unrecorded
Cliff Geyser	40-50 ft.....	2- 3 hours ...	Twice weekly
Comet Geyser	30-60 ft....	1- 5 minutes..	Irregular
Daisy Geyser	75 feet....	3- 4 minutes..	1½-3 hours
Dragon Geyser	15-20 ft....	3- 5 minutes..	(Dormant)
Economic Geyser Crater	10-20 ft.....	10 seconds..	(Dormant)
Fan Geyser	6-100 feet....	5-10 minutes..	With Mortar Gey.
Giant Geyser	150-180 feet	1½ hours.......	6-16 days
Giantess Geyser	150-200 ft....	12-36 hours ...	Seldom
Grand Geyser	180-200 ft....	30-45 minutes..	20-80 hours
Green Spring	20 feet....	5 minutes..	1-3 hours
Grotto Geyser	20-30 ft.....	1 hour....	2-8 hours
Infant Geyser	Few feet....	Unrecorded ...	(Dormant)
Jewel Geyser	12-22 ft....	1-1.5 minutes..	5-10 minutes
Lion Geyser	50-60 ft.....	2- 4 minutes..	6-15 times daily
Lioness Geyser	80 feet....	10 minutes..	(Dormant)
Little Cub Geyser	3-10 ft.....	17 minutes..	1-2 hours
Mastiff Geyser	Few feet....	Varies	Frequent
Midget Geyser	30 feet....	Unrecorded ...	Seldom
Model Geyser	3-4 feet...	Unrecorded ...	Unrecorded
Mortar Geyser	30 feet....	6- 8 minutes..	With Fan Geyser
Oblong Geyser	20-40 ft....	6- 9 minutes..	5-8 hours
Old Faithful Geyser ...	116-171 ft....	4 minutes..	66.3 minutes
Pump Geyser	3 feet....	Few seconds..	Few seconds
Rainbow Pool	40 feet....	10 minutes..	(Dormant)
Restless Geyser	3 feet....	Almost steady.	Almost steady
Riverside Geyser	80-100 ft....	15 minutes.	6-9½ hours
Rocket Geyser	10 feet....	2- 3 minutes..	2-5 hours
Sapphire Pool	4-12 ft.....	2 minutes..	10-20 minutes
Sawmill Geyser	17-32 ft.....	1- 3 hours ..	3 hours
Sentinel Geysers	20 feet....	Unrecorded ...	2-3 days
Solitary Geyser	25 feet....	2 minutes..	2-6 minutes

GEYSERS AT UPPER GEYSER BASIN—Concluded

Name	Height	Duration	Interval
Spa Geyser	50 feet....	Unrecorded ...	Seldom
Spanker Geyser	3 inches....	Perpetual.....	None
Spasmodic Geyser	15 feet....	20-60 minutes..	1 or 2 daily
Splendid Geyser	125-150 ft....	10 minutes..	Seldom
Sponge Geyser	6 inches....	1 minute......	45 seconds
Spouter Geyser	3- 6 ft.....	30-40 minutes..	1 or 2 daily
Sprinkler Geyser	Several ft....	3- 5 minutes..	Daily
Surprise Geyser	100 feet....	2 minutes..	Irregular
Tardy Geyser	3 feet....	30 minutes......	2-3 hours
Terra Cotta Spring	3 feet....	Varies	3 or 4 daily
Three Sisters Springs..	4 feet....	Varies	Occasional
Turban Geyser	20 feet....	4-10 hours....	15-22 minutes
Whistle Geyser	40 feet....	30 minutes..	(Dormant)
White Geyser	Unrecorded .	Unrecorded ...	Unrecorded

UPPER GEYSER BASIN (OLD FAITHFUL)

14.00   2.20   **Biscuit Basin** named for the geyserite knobs around Sapphire Pool and other hot springs in this part of Upper Geyser Basin, is traversed by a short spur road to the parking area at Firehole River, a footbridge and path. Near the main road are **Cauliflower Geyser** whose eruptions are only vigorous boiling, and **Mirror Pool.**

Sapphire Pool which boils up every 10 to 20 minutes to a height of 4 to 12 feet, is across the river (west), as are: **Jewel Geyser** which erupts every 5 to 10 minutes to a height of 12 to 22 feet, **Shell Spring, Silver Globe Spring, Avoca Spring** and **Mustard Springs.**

About a mile distant at the south are **Hillside Springs** of which **Asta Spring** is the only one named. Unlike most of the other sinter deposited in Up-

per, Midway and Lower geyser basins (nearly pure hydrous silica—geyserite), the deposits from the Hillside Springs are a mixture of calcareous and silicious sinters.

14.30   1.90   **Gem Pool is** west of and near the road.

14.40   1.80   The large geyser crater below the road is **Artemisia Geyser** which erupts every 24 to 30 hours, 15 to 35 feet high for 10 to 25 minutes. Near by is **Atomizer Geyser** which erupts about once each day, duration one minute, maximum height 20 feet; and **Restless Geyser** is 60 feet nearer the river.

14.68   1.52   **Sentinel Geysers** are on both sides of the Firehole River at this point. They erupt every 2 to 3 days about 20 feet in height.

14.75   1.45   Between the road and the river is **Morning Glory Pool,** considered one of the most beautiful blue pools in the park. Its deep blue color

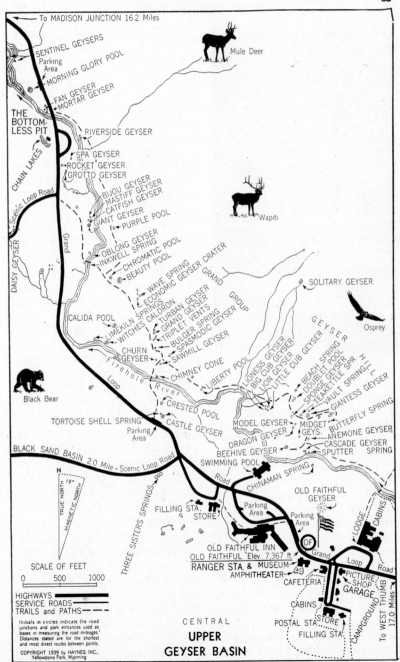

To MADISON JUNCTION 16.2 Miles

SENTINEL GEYSERS
Parking Area
MORNING GLORY POOL
FAN GEYSER
MORTAR GEYSER
THE BOTTOMLESS PIT
RIVERSIDE GEYSER
SPA GEYSER
ROCKET GEYSER
GROTTO GEYSER
BIJOU GEYSER
MASTIFF GEYSER
CATFISH GEYSER
GIANT GEYSER
PURPLE POOL
OBLONG GEYSER
INKWELL SPRING
CHROMATIC POOL
BEAUTY POOL
WAVE SPRING
ECONOMIC GEYSER CRATER
LIMEKILN SPRINGS
URBAN GEYSER
WITCHES CALDRON
GRAND GEYSER
TRIPLET VENTS
BULGER SPRING
SPASMODIC GEYSER
CHURN GEYSER
SAWMILL GEYSER
CHIMNEY CONE
LIBERTY POOL

CALIDA POOL

Chain Lakes
Scenic Loop Road
Grand
Firehole
Loop
River

DAISY GEYSER

SOLITARY GEYSER

Osprey

G E Y S E R G R O U P

LIONESS GEYSER
BIG CUB GEYSER
LION GEYSER
LITTLE CUB GEYSER
BEACH SPRING
DOUBLET POOL
SPONGE GEYSER
TEAKETTLE SPR.
VAULT SPRING
GIANTESS GEYSER
BUTTERFLY SPRING

Black Bear

TORTOISE SHELL SPRING
Parking Area
CASTLE GEYSER
CRESTED POOL

MODEL GEYSER
MIDGET GEYS.
DRAGON III
BEEHIVE GEYSER
SWIMMING POOL
ANEMONE GEYSER
CASCADE GEYSER
SPUTTER SPRING

BLACK SAND BASIN 2.0 Mile - Scenic Loop Road

CHINAMAN SPRING

OLD FAITHFUL GEYSER

LODGE
CABINS

THREE SISTERS SPRINGS

FILLING STA.
STORE
Parking Area
Parking Area

Road
Grand
Loop
Road

OLD FAITHFUL INN
OLD FAITHFUL Elev. 7,367 ft.
RANGER STA. & MUSEUM
AMPHITHEATER
CAFETERIA
CABINS
POSTAL STA.
STORE
FILLING STA.

PICTURE SHOP
GARAGE
CAMPGROUND

To WEST THUMB 17.0 Miles

Mule Deer

Wapiti

N
TRUE NORTH 19°
MAGNETIC NORTH

SCALE OF FEET
0   500   1000

HIGHWAYS
SERVICE ROADS
TRAILS and PATHS

Initials in circles indicate the road
junctions and park entrances used as
bases in measuring the road mileages.
Distances stated are for the shortest
and most direct routes between points.

COPYRIGHT 1939 by HAYNES INC.,
Yellowstone Park, Wyoming

C E N T R A L
UPPER
GEYSER BASIN

RIVERSIDE GEYSER

is seen only when the blue sky is reflected in its transparent water. It is photographed most successfully at midday when its depths are lighted and the amount of steam rising is at a minimum.

14.80   1.40   Between the road and the river are **Fan** and **Mortar** geysers, which have subterranean connections. They erupt together for 5 to 10 minutes, the Fan to a height of 100 feet, the Mortar 30 feet, but only a few times each season.

14.85   1.35   Firehole River crossing. East of the road across the river is the cone of **Riverside Geyser,** which erupts

80 to 100 feet in height every 6 to 9½ hours, eruptions lasting 15 minutes. The water is thrown out at an angle and drops into the river. This is one of the most important and spectacular geysers and should be seen by every park visitor. On the opposite side of the road are **Chain Lakes, The Bottomless Pit** and an unnamed geyser (now dormant) which used to erupt 35 feet high.

14.95   1.25   **Spa Geyser** is between the road and the river. It seldom erupts but when active attains a height of 50 feet.

15.00   1.20   The curious geyser cone near the road is **Grotto Geyser,** which erupts every 2 to 8 hours, 20 to 30 feet in height; duration being an hour. Eruptions of this geyser are very difficult to photograph; the most satisfactory pictures are of the cone when inactive.

15.05   1.15   A scenic loop road, 1.99 miles in length, starts west from here along which are many important features including: Daisy Geyser, Punch Bowl Spring, Black Sand Pool, Sunset Lake, Rainbow Pool and Emerald Pool.

From this junction is seen the broken cone of **Giant Geyser** long reputed to be the highest geyser. Recent measurements reveal its height at 150 to 180 feet. It usually erupts 1½ hours at intervals of from 6 to 16 days; but at times is less regular.

GIANT GEYSER   DAISY GEYSER

BLACK SAND BASIN LOOP

The distances from this junction are given in parentheses following the name of each feature, the north junction being 0.00 miles.

Daisy Geyser at west of road usually erupts every 1½ to 3 hours 75 feet high for 3 to 4 minutes; like the Riverside Geyser the water is ejected at an angle. In this group are also **Bonita Pool, Brilliant Pool, Splendid Geyser Crater** (now dormant), and **Comet Geyser,** which erupts to a height of 30 to 60 feet for 1 to 5 minutes at irregular intervals. A few hundred feet to the northwest is the cone of an extinct geyser, now known as **White Pyramid Geyser Cone.** When one considers the fact that even in our short lifetimes many changes have been observed—**new geysers** have come into existence, oth-

ers have become dormant, the ground has blown out and formed new hot springs at a dozen places, and others have dried up—it is not surprising that many areas are found which are either wholly extinct or are exhaling their last breaths; and while it is true that geysers and hot springs are manifestations of dying volcanic action, the total amount of activity at present is probably only imperceptibly less than it was a century ago. This activity even antedated the glacial period. Geological processes which are still going on are extremely slow. One eminent educator, Dr. Ray Lyman Wilbur, when he was Secretary of the Interior, referred to these springs at Upper Geyser Basin as "live geology". **Punch Bowl Spring** (0.39 mi.) is at the right of the road on the mound. **Black**

CASTLE GEYSER

Sand Pool (0.59 mi.) at the right is a large hot spring which overflows, covering quite a large area between it and **Iron Creek**, a tributary of the Firehole River, to the west. **Algal Pool** (0.94 mi.) at the right shows good examples of the built-up mushroom type of deposit. **Spouter Geyser** (0.96

mi.) at the right usually boils rather violently to a height of 3 to 6 feet for 30 to 40 minutes once or twice daily. The overflow from Sunset Lake produces a beautiful display of algae coloring. Parking area and footbridge over Iron Creek (0.99 mi.). At the right is the crater of **Cliff Geyser** which erupts about twice weekly 40 to 50 feet high.

The near by once famous **Handkerchief Pool** could not stand the abuse given it; it is filled with surface material, and dry.

Rainbow Pool erupted twice daily for 10 minutes to a maximum height of 40 ft., in 1940, was quiescent in 1941, but played in 1942.

Sunset Lake is a large hot lake with a beautifully colored basin and runways. A few hundred feet to the south is **Emerald Pool**, a large, quiescent, crystal clear basin of hot water of beautiful green color.

Dr. Arthur Nash, former ranger naturalist, is quoted regarding algae:

"I find from my data that when I collected from Emerald Pool the temperature of the water was 69.5° (Centigrade). There were three plants present. One, a unicellular alga which I named Gloeothece Yellowstonense, is abundant in the samples. Another is Phormidium rubrum Tilden, a filamentous alga named by Professor Josephine E. Tilden in 1896. This is also abundant. A third one, Phormidium faveolarum (Montagne) Gomont, is also a filamentous alga. It is an older form, and this last one is less common in the samples. All are blue-green algae, known as Cyanophyceae."

Green Spring usually quiet, erupted during late 1941 every 1 to 3 hours 20 feet high.

Whistle Geyser (1.04 mi.) at north of road has been observed to erupt 40 feet high for 30 minutes, but is now dormant.

Three Sisters Springs (1.89 mi.) is a chain lake group of five hot springs, one of which erupts 5 feet high at times. (1.94 mi.) occasional puffs of steam are seen in the distance ahead on the hillside. These come from **Solitary Geyser,** which erupts 25 feet high for 2 minutes every 2 to 6 minutes. The scenic loop road (south end 1.99 mi.) joins The Grand Loop Road at this point. Between here and the north end of the scenic loop road, along The Grand Loop Road which follows the Firehole River, are Castle Geyser and Tortoise Shell Spring.

GRAND LOOP ROAD

15.70   0.50 Parking area. **Castle Geyser,** one of the oldest geysers in the park, erupts 65 to 100 ft. high for 25 to 30 minutes every 24 to 30 hours, but after a few eruptions have occurred this geyser quiets down and rests for a few days before starting another series of eruptions. During this rest period it occasionally throws out single spurts 10 to 15 feet high, but these must not be mistaken for the regular eruptions of this magnificent geyser. At the northwest side of Castle Geyser is **Tortoise Shell Spring**, with a beautifully beaded crater, of extremely hot and violently agitated water. Between here and the Firehole River something over 100 feet from Castle Geyser is **Crested Pool.** Near the riverbank and downstream about 500 feet is **Terra Cotta Spring** which erupts 3 or 4 times daily 3 feet high.

Spanker Geyser further downstream is a perpetual spouter erupting 3 feet high.

Witches Caldron on the opposite bank of Firehole River is a quiet hot spring.

15.80   0.40 Junction, south end of Black Sand Basin side loop road.

15.90   0.30 Side road leads to filling station and general store operated by Hamilton Stores, Inc.

16.00   0.20 East of the road is a large **swimming pool** operated by C. A. Hamilton, and on the opposite side is **Old Faithful Inn**, the main part of which was opened in 1904 but since that time two large wings, an enlarged dining room, and other additions have been built to accommodate increasing patronage.

16.20   0.00 **Old Faithful Geyser** is at the east of the road. Marker on concrete post gives elevation as 7,367 feet. Since the time when this geyser was named in 1870 by Surv. Gen. H. D. Washburn, leader of the expedition of that year, it has erupted more than half a million times. By measurement its height varies from 116 to 171 feet, the average interval is 66.3 minutes and the duration of each eruption 4 minutes.

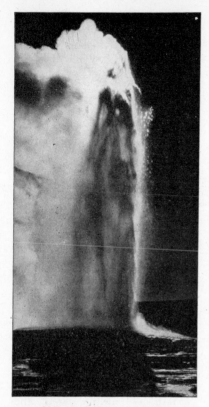

OLD   FAITHFUL   GEYSER

No two eruptions are alike or even similar. The first high shaft of the eruption is not its greatest one but most people photograph this first display and are changing the film about the time the geyser attains its maximum height. From 10,000 to 12,000 gallons of water are discharged at each eruption, yet this is not the greatest geyser in point of size in the park as it is eclipsed by the Grand Geyser, which erupts from 180 to 200 feet in height, and the Giant Geyser previously mentioned.

It is, however, the greatest geyser in point of popularity and regularity. Like all geysers Old Faithful erupts without regard for its public. It performs day and night, summer and winter. As in the case of almost all of the cold and hot springs the world over, the source of the water of Old Faithful Geyser is almost entirely meteoric (from rain and snow). The sources of both the water and the heat are so deep-seated that only slight changes are noted during the various seasons of the year in its regularity, height, and the amount of water discharged. All geysers are affected by periods of drouth but the heat, which comes from the central heat of the earth, apparently does not vary. Premonitory cannonading characteristic of many geysers is heard usually before eruptions begin in earnest. This is caused by the collapse of steam bubbles underground in the geyser tube. Many theories as to the eruptive force of gey-

After dark one eruption is usually illuminated by a giant searchlight. This is undoubtedly the most photographed geyser in the world. A common error made by first-timers is to try to photograph the geyser from a position too close to it. Most photographs show the top or the bottom or the middle, but not all three. It not only erupts to an average height of 150 feet, but steam clouds rise from this column of scalding water to a height of 1,000 feet or more when the air is still.

OLD FAITHFUL INN

sers seem to be quite inadequate in explaining all the various types of eruptions. An elementary principle probably involved in both simple and complex geysers is suggested from observing a geyser m o d e l. Since the source of heat is constant and the column of water underground, after the tube is filled, remains practically stationary, it becomes steadily hotter. As soon as the pressure due to the weight of the water in the lower reaches of the tube is relieved by the first spurt of an eruption, the column of water starts upward and the pressure of its weight on the lower part is momentarily lessened. This causes a great flash of steam from the superheated water and it is this explosion that hurls the scalding water into the air.

The **museum** and **amphitheater** (where lectures are held daily during the travel season), are on the opposite side of the road from Old Faithful Geyser. The museum contains very interesting exhibits pertaining largely to geysers and hot springs. The ranger naturalists of the National Park Service, who conduct hikes and motor caravans throughout this area, operate the information desk, and give the lectures in the amphitheater headquarter here.

The **Ranger Station** is in the museum building.

Old Faithful Lodge is situated east of Old Faithful Geyser. The lodge consists of a large central building, a spacious recreation hall, and a large number of furnished cabins. Between the **campground** and Old Faithful Geyser are the cafeteria, cabin headquarters and a large group of cabins, a general store and filling station (both operated by Hamilton Stores, Inc.), a Haynes Picture Shop, garage, woodyard, and other facilities.

Chinaman Spring, normally quiescent, once erupted 40 feet when a laundryman put soap into it. Soap may cause certain types of hot springs to erupt; but that practice is no longer permitted.

Observation Point overlooking the south end of Upper Geyser Basin is about 100 feet above the flat and is reached by path starting from a footbridge over the Firehole River.

GEYSER HILL

The features on Geyser Hill are shown on the map, page 83. This area is on the opposite side of Firehole River from Old Faithful Geyser and is traversed by a footpath.

Downstream from the footbridge near the north bank of the river are **Sputter Spring** and **Cascade Geyser** (dormant) which formerly erupted at times 30 feet high.

The footpath leading to the Giantess Geyser Crater passes near several small features including **Anemone Geyser** which erupts frequently a few feet high, **Midget Geyser** rarely in eruption, but 30 feet high, **Dragon Geyser** (d o r m a n t) which formerly erupted 15 to 20 feet high and **Model Geyser** which sometimes erupts 3 to 4 feet high but is not often active.

Giantess Geyser, one of the most tremendous of all, erupts from 150 to 200 feet high in a series of upheavals lasting from 12 to 36 hours accompanied by subterranean c a n n o n a d - ing which shakes the ground for hundreds of feet around the crater. Eruptions formerly 10 to 20 days apart now occur at much longer intervals.

At the east are some unnamed large hot springs and the sinter-filled craters of the now extinct **Butterfly Spring**.

Between the Giantess and Lion groups are **Vault Spring, Teakettle Spring, The Pump** (a crater), **Topaz Spring** (dry in 1941), **Sponge Geyser** which erupts a few inches high for a minute with 45-second intervals, **Doublet Pool** with horizontal sheets of geyserite partly covering the pool, **Beach Spring** which erupts 2 feet high every 2 to 3 hours, **Ear Spring** named for its shape, and **Goggles Spring** a good example of intermittent hot springs.

Lion Geyser when active, erupts 50 to 60 feet high for 2 to 4 minutes 6 to 15 times daily at intervals ½ to 2 hours apart. **Lioness Geyser** and **Big Cub Geyser** are both dormant. **Lit-**

tle Cub Geyser erupts every 1 to 2 hours for 17 minutes, 3 to 10 feet high.

Beehive Geyser near the lower path returning to the footbridge erupts 200 to 219 feet high for 2 to 8 minutes but in recent seasons has been seen in action very seldom.

* * *

The path continues northwest to a footbridge near the Saw Mill Geyser and another near Oblong Geyser. Nearly 2000 feet up the slope is Solitary Geyser which erupts 25 feet high for 2 minutes every 2 to 6 minutes. Along the level path are Liberty Pool, Chimney Cone (dormant) near the river, Saw Mill Geyser which erupts 17 to 32 feet high for 1 to 3 hours every 3 hours, Tardy Geyser eruptions of which occur every 2 to 3 hours, last 30 minutes and are 3 feet high, Churn Geyser, Spasmodic Geyser which erupts 15 feet high once or twice daily to a height of 15 feet, Bulger Spring which erupts 3 to 7 feet high about once a day, and Triplet Vents.

Grand Geyser erupts 180 to 200 feet high in a series of displays lasting 30 to 45 minutes every 20 to 80 hours. Turban Geyser erupts with Grand Geyser 20 feet high and at other times only 6 feet high at 17 minute intervals.

Near the riverbank are Witches Caldron and Limekiln Springs and closer to the path is Calida Pool.

Economic Geyser Crater and Wave Spring are both dormant.

Beauty Pool and Chromatic Pool at intervals of 3 to 5 weeks alternately ebb and flow, one receding while the other overflows.

Upstream from the footbridge on the west bank is Inkwell Spring exhibiting black algae, further on is Oblong Geyser which erupts 20 to 40 feet high for 6 to 9 minutes every 5 to 8 hours—a beautiful crater.

Giant Geyser as previously noted, erupts 150 to 180 feet high usually at intervals of 6 to 16 days, duration 1½ hours.

On the same mound with the Giant are Bijou Geyser small and erupting almost steadily, Catfish Geyser erupting 8 feet high most of the time, and Mastiff Geyser which erupts only a few feet high but frequently.

UPPER GEYSER BASIN to WEST THUMB GEYSER BASIN

The Grand Loop Road from Upper Geyser Basin to West Thumb Junction, on West Thumb Bay of Yellowstone Lake covers a distance of 17.00 miles. High lights of this section of The Grand Loop Road are: Kepler Cascades, a side spur 2.5 miles in length to Lone Star Geyser, the crossing of the Continental Divide through Craig Pass (in which is Isa Lake whose waters flow to both the Atlantic and Pacific oceans), a second crossing of the Continental Divide and a high view of both Yellowstone Lake and the Absaroka Range, just before reaching West Thumb Junction.

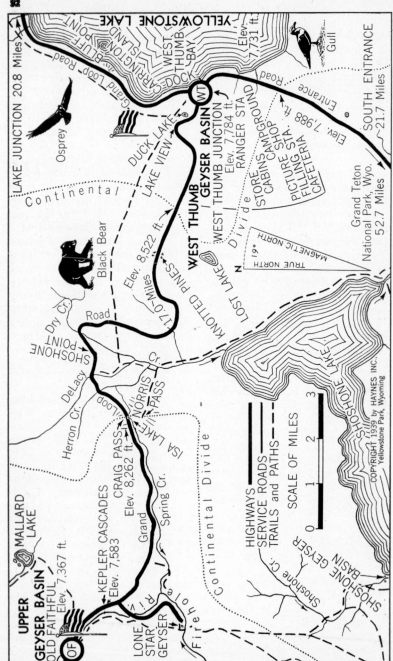

YELLOWSTONE LAKE

WEST THUMB BAY

CARRINGTON ISLAND POINT

BLUFF POINT

Grand Loop Road

LAKE JUNCTION 20.8 Miles

Osprey

Gull

Elev. 7,731 ft.

WEST THUMB DOCK

WT

WEST THUMB / GEYSER BASIN JUNCTION

Elev. 7,784 ft.
RANGER STA.

Elev. 7,988 ft.

STORE
CABINS
PICTURE STA.
CAFETERIA

CAMPGROUND
SHOP
FILLING STA.

Entrance Road

SOUTH ENTRANCE 21.7 Miles

Grand Teton National Park, Wyo. 52.7 Miles

WEST THUMB / GEYSER BASIN

Continental

Lake View

Duck Lake

Black Bear

Elev. 8,522 ft.

1.0 Miles

Knotted Pines

Lost Lake

Divide

TRUE NORTH
MAGNETIC NORTH
19°
N

Dry Cr.

Road

Shoshone Point

Cr.

Norris Pass

DeLacy

Herron Cr.

Isa Lake

Grand Loop

Craig Pass
Elev. 8,262 ft.

Spring Cr.

Continental Divide

Shoshone Cr.

SHOSHONE LAKE

COPYRIGHT 1939 by HAYNES INC.
Yellowstone Park, Wyoming

HIGHWAYS
SERVICE ROADS
TRAILS and PATHS

SCALE OF MILES

0   1   2   3

UPPER GEYSER BASIN

MALLARD LAKE

OLD FAITHFUL
Elev. 7,367 ft.

KEPLER CASCADES
Elev. 7,583

OF

LONE STAR GEYSER

Firehole River

SHOSHONE GEYSER BASIN

0.00   17.00   **Old Faithful**
(elevation at concrete post
near the geyser is 7,367 feet).
The starting mileage at the
west end of this leg of the trip
is taken at a point on the highway in line with Old Faithful
Geyser and the museum.

0.07   16.93   South of the
road are the cafeteria, cabin
headquarters, a large group of
cabins, general store and filling
station, campground, garage
and other facilities.

0.08   16.92   Haynes Picture
Shop on the campground side
of the road.

0.20   16.80   Lodge main
building, recreation building
and a large group of furnished
cabins are north of the road.

0.40   16.60   Firehole River
crossing.

0.65   16.35   Trail leads
to **Mallard Lake** at the northeast about 3.5 miles.

1.00   16.00   Western skyline
is the **Madison Plateau**, which
extends north and south from
the Madison River to the valley
of the Bechler River, in the
southwest corner of the park.

1.60   15.40   **Kepler Cascades** of the Firehole River are
a series of falls 100 to 150 feet
in height, between perpendicu-
lar canyon walls. (The elevation near the highway at this
point is 7,583 feet.)

The true **forget-me-not** (My-
osotis) grows only in the higher
altitudes in the park, although
similar flowers are common
throughout the region. It is a
low plant, the flowers being
usually pale blue, though in
some cases dark blue, and its
leaves are small and softly
hairy. The name is from **the**
words "mouse" and "ear," **de-**
scribing the leaves.

1.70   15.30   Side spur, **2.5**
miles in length (round **trip 5**
miles) leads up the Firehole
River to Lone Star Geyser.

LONE STAR GEYSER SPUR

At the side of the spur **road**
is a dam in the Firehole **River**
for the water supply of the village at Upper Geyser Basin
(0.20 mi.); cross Firehole **River**
(0.54); the abandoned crossing
of Firehole River and mouth **of**
Spring Creek, an eastern **trib-**
utary of Firehole River, rising
in Isa Lake (1.61 mi.); keep
left (2.03 mi.), right side road
is a wood road; parking **area**
and turn around at Lone Star
Geyser and geyser basin (**2.48**
mi.). A trail to Shoshone Lake
and Shoshone Geyser Basin at
the southeast, meets the **road**
at this point. This trail forks,
one leg going down the Bechler
River to the southwest corner
of the park; the other leg going
around the south side of Shoshone Lake, past Lewis and
Heart lakes to Snake River.

The geyserite cone of **Lone
Star Geyser** is 10 to 12 feet high
and as large in diameter. During
eruptions which are 25 feet in
height and last 10 minutes at
intervals of 20 minutes to 3
hours (the higher eruptions following the usual interval of 3
hours), water is ejected through
a group of small orifices in the
top of the cone.

Shoshone Geyser Basin, at the west end of Shoshone Lake is reached only by trail. It is 5 miles (air-line) almost directly south of Lone Star Geyser. The principal geysers in this large thermal area are listed (See geyser table) but in addition there are a great many hot springs and vents in this geyser basin.

GRAND LOOP ROAD

3.95   13.05   An unnamed pond is north of the road.

4.10   12.90   A glacial lake is at the north.

4.30   12.70   Spring Creek crossing. Pond south of road.

6.20   10.80   A patch of colorful altered rhyolite at the north of the road owes its coloring to iron oxide, same as is found in the Grand Canyon.

6.35   10.65   To the southeast is **Norris Pass,** through which a trail leads southward to the east shore of Shoshone Lake and thence to the south boundary of the park by way of Heart Lake and along the Snake River.

6.80   10.20   **Isa Lake** at **Craig Pass** on the crest of the **Continental Divide.** (Elevation 8,262 feet.) This little lake drains through Spring Creek to the west, finally reaching the Atlantic Ocean at the Gulf of Mexico by way of the Firehole, Madison, Missouri and Mississippi rivers. The rivulet starting east finds its way through Herron Creek to Shoshone and Lewis lakes, thence to the Pacific Ocean (south of Puget Sound) by way of the Lewis, Snake and Columbia rivers.

7.15   9.85   Colorful altered rhyolite in bank.

7.60   9.40   **Herron Creek** crossing. This creek, a tributary of DeLacy Creek, drains into Shoshone Lake, thence to Lewis Lake and Lewis River to the Snake River.

7.90   9.10   **DeLacy Creek** crossing.

GEYSERS AT SHOSHONE GEYSER BASIN

NAME	HEIGHT	DURATION	INTERVAL
Bead Geyser	10–20 ft.....	Unrecorded ...	Unrecorded
Bronze Geyser	1– 3 ft.....	Several seconds	1-2 minutes
Lion Geyser	10-12 ft.....	4 minutes..	Unrecorded
Little Bulger Geyser ..	5–10 ft.....	1.5-2 minutes..	5-6 minutes
Little Giant Geyser ...	10-50 ft.....	13-28 minutes..	2 per day
Minute Man Geyser ...	20 feet....	2.5 minutes..	1-3 minutes
Shield Geyser	2– 4 ft.....	Unrecorded ...	Few seconds*
Small Geyser	2-20 ft.....	1 minute..	2 minutes
Union Geyser:			
Northern Cone** ...	66 feet....	10-13 minutes..	Several per week
Center Cone**	114 feet....	5-60 minutes..	Several per week
Southern Cone**	3 feet....	Few minutes..	Several per week

*When basin is filled with water.
**Eruptions from all three cones occur simultaneously.

ISA LAKE ON THE CONTINENTAL
DIVIDE

8.50   8.50 **Shoshone Point**
affords a view of Shoshone
Lake at the south, which body
of water is nearly 7 miles long.
The Teton Range in Grand Teton National Park, about 50
miles away, may also be seen
from this point on a clear day.

9.00   8.00 **Dry Creek**
crossing.

12.20   4.80 **Knotted pines**
may be seen on both sides of
the road.

13.65   3.35 The **Continental Divide** is crossed at an elevation of 8,522 feet on a rolling plateau.

Lost Lake is about a mile
(air-line) southwest of this
point on the road. It is about a
two hour roundtrip on foot and
requires a guide. Former maps
in error showed this lake on the
east side of the Continental Divide, but it has recently been
determined that it is on the
west side and drains into Shoshone Lake.

Kinnikinnick (Arctostaphy-
los) or bearberry is found in
the undergrowth in the pine
forests. It is a trailing evergreen shrub, having very small
bell-shaped pink or white flowers which are followed later by
dark-red berries. It was named
"bearberry" as the berries provide choice morsels of food for
bruin. "Kinnikinnick" is the
Eastern Indian name for "a mixture" and applies to various
plants where the dried leaves
and bark were mixed and
smoked by the Indians and pioneers, prior to the general use
of tobacco.

15.20   1.80 The small evergreen plant growing on the
floor of the forest is dwarf
huckleberry.

16.00   1.00 **Lake View**.
From here is had a magnificent
view of Yellowstone Lake and
the distant Absaroka Range to
the east. The Cook-Folsom
diary (trip of 1869) quoted:

"We ascended the summit of a
neighboring hill and took a final
look at Yellowstone Lake. Nes-
tled among the forest-crowned hills
which bounded our vision lay this
inland sea, its crystal waves danc-
ing and sparkling in the sunlight
as if laughing with joy for their
wild freedom. It is a scene of tran-
scendant beauty which has been
viewed by but few white men, and
we felt glad to have looked upon it
before its primeval solitude should
be broken by the crowds of pleasure
seekers which at no distant day will
throng its shores."

The Expedition of 1869 was
composed of only three men—
Charles W. Cook, David E. Folsom, and William Peterson. The
names of the first two of these

TETON MOUNTAINS, GRAND TETON NATIONAL PARK

men are perpetuated by Cook Peak and Folsom Peak, in the Washburn Range near Tower Fall.

16.40   0.60   For 0.1 mile the road partly circles **Duck Lake**, the source of the water supply for the village of West Thumb. No fishing is permitted in this lake.

16.90   0.10   The road passes through a pure stand of Engelmann spruce trees.

17.00   0.00   **West Thumb Junction**, elevation 7,784 feet. South of the junction is the village of West Thumb; a general store, filling station, Haynes Picture Shop, ranger station, a group of cabins, campground and cafeteria. At this point the road to South Entrance, 21.7 miles, joins The Grand Loop Road. (West Thumb Geyser Basin will be described immediately following description of the South Entrance Road.)

SOUTH ENTRANCE

The South Entrance of the park is 23.5 miles north of Moran, Wyoming; 31.0 miles north of Grand Teton National Park; and 56.6 miles north of Jackson, Wyo. From Moran, U. S. Highway 287 leads southeast through Togwotee Pass to Dubois, Lander (the western terminus of the Chicago & Northwestern Line), and Rawlins on U. S. 30). The south highway, from which a loop road penetrates Grand Teton National Park, turns west at Jackson and crosses Teton Pass to Pierre's Hole, now known as the Teton Basin, thence to Sugar City, Idaho, on the north-south highway from Salt Lake City to West Yellowstone. From Jackson a highway (U. S. 187) leads southeast to Rock Springs, Wyo., on U. S. 30, and a fork goes almost due south to Kemmerer on U. S. 30 N highway.

Grand Teton National Park established Feb. 26, 1929, includes a range of mountains about 30 miles long and several beautiful bodies of water, of which Jackson Lake is the largest. **Grand Teton Mountain,** the highest pinnacle of the range, is 13,766 feet high. This mountain was one of the best-known landmarks of pioneer days, when Indians resided in this area and trappers were the first white men to penetrate the wilderness in pursuit of their business of killing fur-bearing animals and trading for pelts with the Indians. Among the first of these was **John Colter,** a former member of the Lewis and Clark Expedition, who is reputed to be the first white man to visit what is now Yellowstone National Park. In 1807-8 he traversed this region, crossed Teton Pass, went north through Pierre's Hole, traveled up Conant Creek near the north end of the Teton Range, and entered what is now Yellowstone Park. From the meager descriptions and maps which are available, his course through the present park appears to have been down Coulter Creek, a southern tributary of the Snake River (this creek just south of the park boundary, was named for John M. Coulter, botanist of one of the early Hayden expeditions. **Colter Peak** (10,500 ft.), 5 miles east of the south end of the southeast arm of Yellowstone Lake, was named for John Colter) thence past Lewis Lake and the West Thumb Bay of Yellowstone Lake to the vicinity of the lake outlet. From here he followed along the west side of Yellowstone River, through Hayden Valley, and saw the mud geyser and mud volcano area, or the thermal area at Crater Hills including Sulphur Mountain, thence northwest on the highlands to the Great Trail of the Indians, which crossed the Yellowstone River above Tower Fall. It is interesting to note that he made no mention of having seen the Upper or Lower falls or the part of the Grand Canyon near these falls, which may be explained by the fact that they were hidden in the heavy forest east of his course. After fording the Yellowstone River, he left the present park region near its northeast corner and trekked back, by way of the Shoshone River near Cody, to his base of operations at the mouth of the Big Horn River, where it flows into Yellowstone River. His description of the geysers and sulphurous hot springs led to the name "Colter's Hell" which was applied to the present park region for many years.

Jackson Hole, east of the Teton Range, is the winter habitat and feeding grounds (Federal elk refuge) of the world's largest herd of wapiti (elk), many of which graze in Yellowstone National Park each summer.

Jackson Hole National Monument containing 221,610 acres was established March 16, 1943.

SOUTH ENTRANCE
to
WEST THUMB GEYSER BASIN

This entrance road joins The Grand Loop Road of the Park at West Thumb Junction, 21.7 miles to the north. High lights along this road are Lewis Canyon, Lewis Falls, Lewis Lake, and the crossing of the Continental Divide at an elevation of 7,988 feet, just before reaching West Thumb Geyser Basin at the junction of this entrance road with The Grand Loop Road of the Park.

(NOTE: The first distance figure shown at the beginning of key paragraphs, applies to those traveling in the same direction as the sequence of paragraphs. Those traveling in the opposite direction, read the paragraphs in reverse order and use the second, instead of the first, distance figure.)

0.00   21.70 **South Entrance**, elevation 6,886 feet, is just south of the confluence of the Lewis and Snake rivers. At the checking station here, as at all entrances to the park, **National Park Service** rangers record all vehicles entering and leaving the park, and issue season permits upon payment of the motor vehicle license fees prescribed by the Secretary of the Interior. Firearms are sealed. Dogs are permitted in the park but must be kept on leash or in crates. Upon leaving the park all visitors are requested to report the number of fish caught.

Fish and Fishing. In the Snake and Lewis rivers and other waters near the South

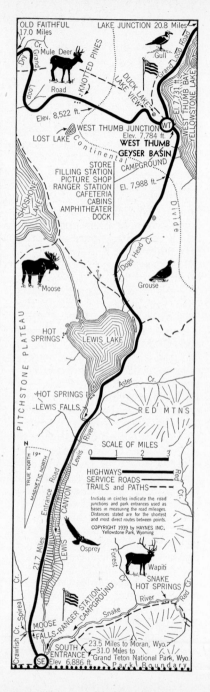

Entrance are the cutthroat trout (redthroat, blackspotted, native), rainbow, Loch Leven, and eastern brook (speckled) trout, and Mackinaw trout (some very large ones having been caught in Lewis Lake). Fishing licenses are not required within the park, but are required in the three states adjoining the park.

0.30 21.40 Campground is on a side road at the east between road and Snake River.

1.40 20.30 **Crawfish Creek** crossing. At the east of the road, in this tributary of the Lewis River is **Moose Falls,** which although not large is very beautiful in its sylvan setting and moss-covered banks.

3.90 17.80 The Teton Range is seen in the distance at the south.

4.20 17.50 South end of **Lewis Canyon.**

4.75 16.95 Several views of Lewis Canyon are had along the 3.15 mile section north of here which follows its rim.

7.75 13.95 Parking area (elevation 7,765 ft.) and view of Lewis Canyon.

7.90 13.80 North end of Lewis Canyon.

8.30 13.40 National Park Service road camp west of the road.

LEWIS FALLS, LEWIS RIVER

10.10 11.60 Lewis River crossing. **Lewis Falls,** about 30 feet high, in the Lewis River is seen at the west.

10.30 11.40 **Aster Creek, a** tributary of the Lewis River, is seen at the east.

11.40 10.30 South end of **Lewis Lake.**

13.85 7.85 View of north end of Lewis Lake.

14.25 7.45 Trail leads eastward to **Heart Lake** and **Heart Lake Geyser Basin** on Witch Creek. (See accompanying geyser table.) This geyser basin is reached only by trail and is visited by few persons.

GEYSERS AT HEART LAKE GEYSER BASIN

Name	Height	Duration	Interval
Deluge Geyser	10-15 ft.....	Unrecorded ...	Unrecorded
Rustic Geyser	30 feet....	1-4 minutes ...	26-90 minutes
Spike Geyser	Unrecorded..	Steady	None

THUMB PAINTPOTS

19.00   2.70   **Continental Divide** crossing at an elevation of 7,988 feet.

21.55   0.15   The **Village of West Thumb.**

21.70   0.00   At **West Thumb Junction,** elevation 7,784 feet, the South Entrance Road joins The Grand Loop Road.

WEST THUMB GEYSER BASIN

Just south of the junction is the **Village of West Thumb** consisting of a cafeteria, ranger station, amphitheater, campground, picture shop, a group of cabins, filling station, general store, boathouse and dock.

GEYSERS AT WEST THUMB GEYSER BASIN

Geysers dormant at time of this revision are included for record.

NAME	HEIGHT	DURATION	INTERVAL
King Geyser	6 feet	10 minutes	Seldom
Lakeshore Geyser	15-25 feet...	10 minutes ...	35 minutes*
Occasional Geyser	25-60 feet...	Unrecorded ...	Irregular
Twin Geysers	Unrecorded.	Unrecorded ...	(Dormant)

*Erupts seldom (2-4 day intervals) when the crater is submerged in the water of the lake.

FISHING CONE, WEST THUMB BAY

Thumb Paintpots and other features in **West Thumb Geyser Basin** (see accompanying geyser table) are at the east between the road and the lake. In addition to the features named in the geyser table are several beautiful hot springs and the celebrated **Fishing Cone**, a hot spring mound surrounded by the water of Yellowstone Lake, except when the lake level is low.

WEST THUMB GEYSER BASIN
to
LAKE (OUTLET)

The next section of The Grand Loop Road is from West Thumb Junction to Lake Junction, a distance of 20.8 miles, the road following the shore of Yellowstone Lake all of the way. High lights are: the north section of West Thumb Geyser Basin in which are a number of unnamed steam vents and hot springs; many enchanting views of the beautiful lake and the peaks of the distant Absaroka Range beyond; and a side spur road, 1.2 miles in length, from Bridge Bay up Bridge Creek to the Natural Bridge.

0.00   20.80   **West Thumb Junction,** elevation 7,784 feet.

1.40   19.40   North end of West Thumb Geyser Basin.

1.95   18.85   **Fisheries Creek** crossing.

2.95   17.85   Highway crosses **Bluff Point.**

3.85   16.95   Near the shore of the lake is **Carrington Island,** a small rocky bird roost, that is submerged when the lake level is high.

5.35   15.45   **Arnica Creek** crossing.

6.40   14.40   Note the natural wave-built sandbar in the lake, which was used as a roadbed for the first road built along this shore of the lake. At the south, about 50 miles away, are seen the peaks of the Teton Range, the highest one being Grand Teton Mountain (13,-766 ft.).

6.95   13.85   East end of sandbar.

8.20   12.60   The **Red Mountains** may be seen 14 miles to the south beyond the south shore of West Thumb Bay. The highest mountain in this group is **Mt. Sheridan** (10,250 ft.) upon the summit of which is a fire lookout.

8.55   12.25   Another view is had of Mt. Sheridan as well as **Flat Mountain** (9,000 ft.) located about 7½ miles northeast of Mt. Sheridan.

10.50   10.30   At this point we are opposite the east boundary of West Thumb Bay, near **Pumice Point.** The small island in Yellowstone Lake is called **Dot Island.**

11.40   9.40   On both sides of the road are mixed stands of Engelmann spruce and lodgepole pine.

11.90   8.90   Many lodgepole pines along the road have been blazed near their bases by porcupines, this bark being one of their staple articles of food.

13.90   6.90   Speedboat excursions for fishing parties are made to **Stevenson Island** from the boathouse near the road east of the fish hatchery.

Cutthroat trout (native, redthroat, blackspotted), practically the only fish which inhabit the lake and its tributaries are caught, and in the shelter house

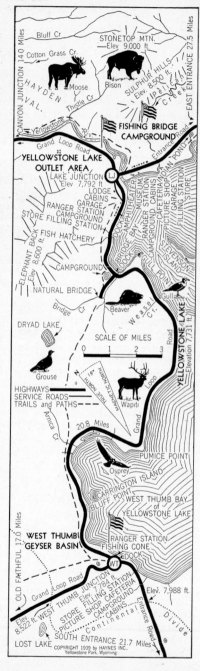

provided by the Yellowstone Park Company on this island, they are fried and served.

Yellowstone Lake is about 20 miles long from north to south and is 14 miles across from West Thumb to the opposite shore of the lake. In shape it has been compared to a disfigured hand, which accounts for the name "West Thumb". Its shore line has been measured at more than 100 miles; and its area computed at 139 square miles. In West Thumb Bay a sounding to a depth of 300 feet has been made, which is the greatest recorded depth of this lake.

In the tree tops all along the lake are nests of eagles and ospreys. A record of a careful count of the **waterfowl** on this lake one fall was given at about 10,000, including a few rare trumpeter swans, many pelicans, great blue herons, Caspian terns, Canadian geese and a large number of ducks of many species, gulls, and other small birds.

The **gull** (sea gull or California gull), a common summer resident in the park, is blue-gray above and white below and has black and white tipped wings. "God-sent" gulls rid "The Promised Land" of a scourge of black crickets which threatened the crops of the Mormons in Utah about the time of the great Mormon migration to the west in the middle of the past century. The gulls rob the industrious merganser of some of the trout it catches, and eat field mice, in-

YELLOWSTONE LAKE AND
COLTER PEAK

sects, and carrion. Travels of banded gulls show that those in the park spend their winters along the coast of California. They arrive in late April or early May and nest in the park on Molly Island in the southeast arm of Yellowstone Lake along with the pelicans and terns, and at many other places at elevations of 7,000 to 8,000 feet.

Swimming in this lake is not encouraged, due to the fact that the water is so cold and the lake is at such a high elevation (7,731 ft.) that even experienced swimmers find swimming difficult on account of the rarity of the air. Those using small boats should exercise great caution as the water is very rough at times, making **boating** extremely hazardous, as such a large body of fresh water (in a given wind) gets much rougher than a body of salt water of similar size, making the use of even large boats impossible at times.

Strange overhead noises at Yellowstone Lake have been reported many times from the earliest days of exploration to the present. These occur when the sky is cloudless, the air perfectly still and usually in early morning. This strange noise, heard only occasionally, is not like the sound of a distant flight of birds nor any shore noise, but is weird and startling. A description of this unusual phenomenon reported by the author in 1924 follows:

"Our small boat was approaching Pelican Roost island. The surface of the lake was mirror-like in the stillness of early morning. A sound rose overhead apparently from the west beginning with a low roar which gradually became louder and rose in pitch, then gradually faded away as the pitch lowered again, while the sound seemed to soar rapidly to the southward as it faded into silence. Then from another direction a similar sound was heard, and again from still another direction, the whole phenomenon lasting only half a minute. Although I am familiar with most of the sounds common to wilderness areas, this was unlike anything I had ever before heard. It was a mystifying sound which none of us in the boat was able to explain. If sound ever accompanied such a display, it is easy to imagine that we had heard the sound effect that would have been used in a stage production of the spectacle of an aurora borealis."

In this connection it might be interesting to relate a story told to the writer by the late John H. Renshawe, who was the geographer in charge of a surveying party of the U. S. Geological Survey at Yellowstone Lake in 1885. Three members of the party were making observations, also in the northeast part of Yellowstone Lake, in a rowboat fitted with a mast and sail. The sky was clear yet the mast was struck by a bolt of lightning, accompanied by a clap of thunder. The oarsman next to the mast was killed and the other men in the boat, including Mr. Renshawe, were rendered unconscious but soon revived and brought their lifeless companion to shore, where other members of the party stated that they had heard the thunder. Mention is made of this tragic incident because it may be possible that the strange overhead sound is of electrical origin, due to the "grounding" of static electricity in the lake from the moisture-laden atmosphere above it.

The shores of this lake were the ancient camping grounds of **Indians.** In building the road along the lake the workmen found many arrowheads, spearheads, skinning knives and other Indian artifacts. Their camps were at a large number of places and it is supposed that they did not reside here the year-round but made excursions to the lake to hunt and fish, when the snow did not prevent travel.

14.05   6.75   **Sand Point** is on the near shore at the south.

14.85   5.95   **Weasel Creek** crossing. Another good view of Stevenson Island is had from here.

15.70   5.10   South edge of **Bridge Bay. Gull Point** extends for quite a distance out into the lake.

16.85   3.95   **Bridge Creek** crossing.

16.90   3.90   West s p u r road to **Natural Bridge** (1.2 mi.).

17.00   3.80   Boathouse and dock. On the opposite side of the road is a campground. At the northeast is seen the **Sleeping Giant**, a reclining figure made by Saddle Mountain and other peaks in the Absaroka Range. Beyond **Gull Point**, at the southeast are three noted peaks (left to right) **Mt. Langford** (10,600 ft.), **Mt. Doane** (10,500 ft.) and **Mt. Stevenson** (10,300 ft.) named for members of the Expedition of 1870.

LAKE (OUTLET)

18.90   1.90   Government boathouse and dock.

19.00   1.80   **Fish Hatchery.** (U. S. Fish and Wildlife Service)—the largest game fish hatchery in the United States.

19.25   1.55   **Lake Hotel** (not open 1947), boathouse.

19.50   1.30   Store and filling station.

19.55   1.25   Ranger Station. South end of side road to the Lake Lodge.

19.90   0.90   **Lake Lodge** and a large group of furnished cabins (also curio and picture shops).

19.95   0.85   North end of loop road to Lake Lodge.

20.70   0.10   A view of Sleeping Giant, outlined in the mountains to the northeast.

20.80   0.00   **Lake Junction,** elevation 7,792 feet.

The **buttercup** (Ranunculus), of which there are many species in the park, grows in moist places, both in the open and partly shaded locations, being numerous near the Grand Canyon and Yellowstone Lake. The attractive yellow flowers bloom in June and July.

FISHING BRIDGE CAMPGROUND

Less than half a mile to the east, across Fishing Bridge over Yellowstone River is the **Fishing Bridge Campground, the** museum, amphitheater, ranger station, cafeteria, cabins, picture shop, repair shop, filling station and store. Boats for fishing are available at the boathouse on the west side of Yellowstone River.

Fishing Bridge. The present Fishing Bridge structure is a few yards downstream from the site of the first celebrated Fishing Bridge, built under the direction of Capt. Hiram Martin Chittenden, of the Corps of Engineers of the U. S. Army, in the summer of 1901, which old bridge served up to midseason 1937, when the new one was completed.

FISHING BRIDGE

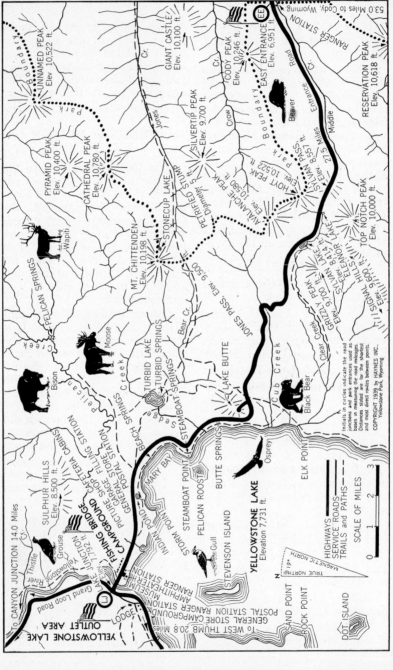

Fishing. All summer long, men, women, and children fish for cutthroat trout in the Yellowstone River from this bridge, which was designed for that purpose as well as for vehicular travel. Surprising as it may seem fishing is good here during most of the season, despite the fact that the bridge has keen competition from the many fishermen who use small boats in the river both above and below this structure.

There is nothing unusual in the stories about some of the trout in Yellowstone Lake being subject to parasites as this condition is common among many species of fish and in many other fishing waters the world over. It is comforting to know that the sizzling frying pan, which brings out the luscious flavor of wild trout, completely destroys the effect of any parasite that might accompany the trout into the pan.

EAST ENTRANCE

Cody, Wyoming (elevation 5,018 ft.), 53.0 miles east of the East Entrance of Yellowstone National Park, was founded in 1897 by Col. Wm. F. Cody (1846-1917), familiarly known as Buffalo Bill. This is a typical Western frontier town, situated on the plains east of the Absaroka Range, of the Rocky Mountains, in which there are many outstanding peaks, one of which, Franks Peak, rises to an elevation of 13,140 feet.

At the edge of Cody are the terminus of the **Burlington Route,** and the **Burlington-Cody Inn,** which are north of the Shoshone River. Buses of the Yellowstone Park Company operate between Cody and the East Entrance, making connections with Burlington Route trains. Near the west edge of the town are **Buffalo Bill Museum,** the **Buffalo Bill Statue** (sculptured by Gertrude Vanderbilt Whitney), and the house which was Col. Cody's boyhood home, moved here from Le Claire, Iowa, his birthplace. Near Cody are **De Maris Springs** and **Shoshone Cavern National Monument,** and in the vicinity are some of the outstanding dude ranches of the west, as well as a large number of cattle and sheep ranches.

On the 53 mile scenic route to the park boundary, 7.6 miles west of Cody at the head of Shoshone Canyon, is **Buffalo Bill Dam,** a tremendous structure 328 feet high and 200 feet wide; at the top it is 10 feet thick and its base, although only 80 feet wide, is 108 feet thick. The dam is between the bases of Rattlesnake Mountain at the north and Cedar Mountain, south of the river. Buffalo Bill often expressed a desire to have his final resting place on Cedar Mountain, which overlooked his favorite hunting ground, but this wish was never realized as his remains are on Lookout Mountain in Colorado. In Buffalo Bill Reservoir, formed by the dam, are impounded the waters of Shoshone River.

Many scenic spots are viewed from this highway, through the Shoshone National Forest, including: Overhanging Rock Cliff, Goose, Holy City, Wooden Shoe, Ptarmigan Mountain, Thors Anvil, Thousand Foot Cliff, The Palisades, Elephant Head, Mutilated Hand, and Chimney Rock, most of which are figures eroded out of rock.

Construction of the road from Yellowstone Lake to Cody was begun in 1890. It was opened to travel in 1903; and in 1912 the first rail passengers entered the park by the East Entrance. The first buses operated over this route were those of the Cody-Sylvan Pass Motor Co. (1916).

The **Shoshone National Forest,** bordering on the park at the east is a part of the first national forest created in the United States (March 30, 1891). The Wapiti ranger station (U. S. Forest Service) north of the road about half way between Cody and East Entrance, is the oldest ranger station in the United States (erected 1903-1904.

EAST ENTRANCE
to
LAKE JUNCTION

This entrance road joins The Grand Loop Road of the Park at Lake Junction, a distance of 27.5 miles from the boundary. High lights of this route are: a climb of more than 1,500 feet in 7½ miles up a broad winding scenic highway to the summit of Sylvan Pass, elevation 8,557 feet; Sylvan Lake; a panoramic

view of Yellowstone Lake from Lake Butte reached by a side road; and Fishing Bridge Campground, just east of Fishing Bridge over Yellowstone River, near Lake Junction.

The East Entrance may be reached via Northwest Airlines to Billings, Montana, thence via the Burlington Route to Cody, Wyoming, and buses of the Yellowstone Park Co.

(NOTE: The first distance figure shown at the beginning of key paragraphs, applies to those traveling in the same direction as the sequence of paragraphs. Those traveling in the opposite direction, read the paragraphs in reverse order and use the second, instead of the first, distance figure.)

0.00   27.50   **East Entrance** checking station, elevation 6,-951 feet   The **National Park Service** rangers at the checking station here, as at all park entrances, record all vehicles entering and leaving the park and issue season permits upon payment of the motor vehicle license fees prescribed by the Secretary of the Interior. Firearms are sealed. Dogs are permitted in the park but must be kept on leash or in crates. Upon leaving the park all visitors are requested to report the number of fish caught.

Fish and Fishing. In the Shoshone River and other waters near the East Entrance are the cutthroat (redthroat, blackspotted, native) trout, eastern brook (speckled) trout, rainbow trout, Rocky Mountain whitefish, some crappies and suckers. No fishing license is required within

TOP NOTCH PEAK AND
SYLVAN LAKE

the park but in Wyoming and the other states adjoining the park state licenses are required.

1.00   26.50   **Middle Creek** at the south of road.

7.00   20.50   Middle Creek Canyon south of road.

7.50   20.00   **Sylvan Pass,** elevation 8,557 feet. **Hoyt Peak** (10,552 ft.) north of road.

8.30   19.20   **Lake Eleanor.**

9.90   17.60   **Sylvan Lake,** elevation 8,414 feet. **Top Notch Peak** (10,000 ft.) across lake in southeast distance. **Avalanche Peak** (10,580 ft.) north of road.

10.70   16.80   **Grizzly Peak** (9,700 ft.) south of road.

11.80   15.70   **Teton Point.** On a clear day the Teton Mountains of which the Grand Teton Mountain (13,766 ft.) is the highest, may be seen at the south, nearly 60 miles away.

13.30   14.20   **C u b   C r e e k** crossing. Cub Creek Campground is nearby.

15.90   11.60   View of Yellowstone Lake.

16.70   10.80   The trail from the upper Yellowstone River at the south crosses the road here.

17.50   10.00   **Lake Butte** side road. This side road leads northeast 0.9 mile to a lookout point on Lake Butte where a splendid view may be had of Yellowstone Lake, the Gallatin Range including Electric Peak in the northwest section of the park, the Red Mountains including Mt. Sheridan in the south center of the park, and the peaks of the Teton Range in Grand Teton National Park nearly 60 miles away.

20.60   6.90   **Pelican Roost,** a small rocky island in Yellowstone Lake near its east shore.

20.70   6.80   S t e a m b o a t Springs on **Steamboat Point.**

21.60   5.90   Holmes Point at the right, south edge of **Mary Bay.** (Carved in a hard rock near the shore are the recently discovered initials of W. H. Holmes, a member of the Hayden Survey of 1871.)

23.60   3.90   Northwest edge of Mary Bay. Steamboat Point is in the southeast distance.

24.20   3.30   South road to **Indian Pond** (sometimes called Squaw Lake). **Concretion Cove** at the south.

24.25   3.25   Old road from **Turbid Lake** joins the main road.

24.40   3.10   Indian Pond south of road.

24.50   3.00   **Sulphur Hills** at the north.

24.90   2.60   South road to Indian Pond.

25.85   1.65   **Pelican Creek** crossing.

FISHING BRIDGE CAMPGROUND

26.70   0.80   East edge of **Fishing Bridge Campground.** In this campground are a large number of camp sites, a bathhouse, ranger station, museum, amphitheater, store, filling station, automobile repair shop, woodyard, picture shop, cabin headquarters, a large group of cabins, and a cafeteria. This is one of the most popular campgrounds in the park. The favorite pastimes here are boating, fishing, beach bathing, and photographing. Myriads of **waterfowl** frequent this lake and afford good opportunities to observe bird life, often including the rare trumpeter swans, and the more common large birds such as pelicans, swans, Canadian geese, great blue herons, as well as eagles, ospreys and

SPEEDBOAT PARTY AND FISHERMEN NEAR YELLOWSTONE LAKE (OUTLET)

FISHING BRIDGE MUSEUM

other hawks; also many smaller birds including gulls, plover, snipe, and almost all species of ducks. In this region, on land, are found moose, wapiti, mule deer and an occasional bison, and along the Yellowstone River are seen beavers and muskrats.

An historic trail from here follows down the east side of the Yellowstone River to the Grand Canyon; a branch leading westward includes a ford across Yellowstone River upstream from the Mud Volcano, which was used by the Indians in the early days.

27.20   0.30 East end of **Fishing Bridge.**

27.25   0.25   Yellowstone River crossing (center of bridge).

27.30   0.20 West end of Fishing Bridge. Parking area and boathouse at north.

27.50   0.00 **Lake Junction** (elevation 7,792 feet), where the entrance road joins The Grand Loop Road of the Park.

(NOTE: For information about Yellowstone Lake and Fishing Bridge please turn back a few pages to the descriptions of the trip from West Thumb to Lake Junction.)

LAKE JUNCTION to GRAND CANYON

From Lake Junction to Canyon Junction, 14.0 miles, The Grand Loop Road follows the Yellowstone River all of the way. High lights of this section of the road are splendid views of the Yellowstone River through the entire length of Hayden Valley; thermal features of importance, including Mud Volcano, Dragons Mouth, and Sulphur Caldron; the course of the road lies through

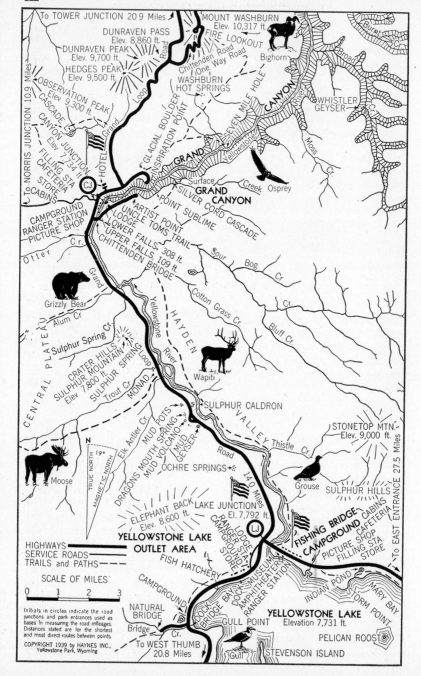

To TOWER JUNCTION 20.9 Miles

MOUNT WASHBURN
Elev. 10,317 ft.

DUNRAVEN PASS
Elev. 8,860 ft.

FIRE LOOKOUT

DUNRAVEN PEAK
Elev. 9,700 ft.

Chittenden Road
(One Way Road)

Bighorn

HEDGES PEAK
Elev. 9,500 ft.

WASHBURN
HOT SPRINGS

WHISTLER
GEYSER

OBSERVATION PEAK
Elev. 9,300 ft.

SEVEN MILE HOLE

Moss Cr.

CANYON JUNCTION
Elev. 7,734 ft.

GLACIAL BOULDER
INSPIRATION POINT

HOTEL

CJ

Surface Creek

GRAND
CANYON

Osprey

CAMPGROUND
RANGER STATION
PICTURE SHOP

ARTIST POINT
POINT SUBLIME

SILVER CORD CASCADE

UNCLE TOMS TRAIL
LODGE

Otter Cr.

LOWER FALLS, 308 ft.
UPPER FALLS, 109 ft.
CHITTENDEN BRIDGE

Spur

Bog Cr.

Grizzly Bear

Grand

Cotton Grass Cr.

Bluff Cr.

Alum Cr.

Yellowstone River

HAYDEN

Sulphur Spring Cr.

CRATER HILLS
SULPHUR MOUNTAIN
Elev. 7,800 ft.

SULPHUR SPRING LOOP

MONAD.

Trout Cr.

Wapiti

SULPHUR CALDRON

VALLEY

STONETOP MTN.
Elev. 9,000 ft.

Thistle Cr.

CENTRAL PLATEAU

Elk Antler Cr.

MUD POTS
MUD SPRING
MUD VOLCANO
MUD GEYSER

Road

140 Miles

Moose

DRAGONS MOUTH SPRING

OCHRE SPRINGS

Grouse

SULPHUR HILLS

N
TRUE NORTH
MAGNETIC NORTH
19°

ELEPHANT BACK
Elev. 8,600 ft.

LAKE JUNCTION
El. 7,792 ft.

LODGE
RANGER STA.
CAMPGROUND
STORE

LJ

FISHING BRIDGE
CAMPGROUND CABINS
PICTURE SHOP
CAFETERIA
FILLING STA.
STORE

YELLOWSTONE LAKE
OUTLET AREA

HIGHWAYS
SERVICE ROADS
TRAILS and PATHS

SCALE OF MILES

0   1   2   3

FISH HATCHERY

CAMPGROUND

Fish Hatchery

DOC MUSEUM
AMPHITHEATER
RANGER STATION

Indian Pond

To EAST ENTRANCE 27.5 Miles

MARY BAY

STORM POINT

Initials in circles indicate the road
junctions and park entrances used as
bases in measuring the road mileages.
Distances stated are for the shortest
and most direct routes between points.

COPYRIGHT 1939 by HAYNES INC.
Yellowstone Park, Wyoming

NATURAL
BRIDGE

Bridge Cr.

To WEST THUMB
20.8 Miles

DOCK
BRIDGE BAY

GULL POINT

Gull

YELLOWSTONE LAKE
Elevation 7,731 ft.

PELICAN ROOST

STEVENSON ISLAND

the summer range for big game animals; on a 1.6 mile scenic side road, the crossing of Yellowstone River on Chittenden Bridge affords a wonderful view of Upper Falls (109 ft.) thence past Canyon Lodge to Artist Point, on the south rim of the Grand Canyon of the Yellowstone, from which is seen the 308 foot Lower Falls. Returning to the main road the route lies past a settlement including picture shop, ranger station, general store and filling station, campground and cafeteria, to Canyon Junction, a short distance from which are Canyon Hotel, and many points from which admirable views of the falls and canyon may be had.

0.00   14.00 **Lake Junction,** elevation 7,792 feet. The route is northwest to the Grand Canyon of the Yellowstone (14 miles).

0.45   13.55 The Grand Loop Road is on one of the terraces of the ancient lake, when it was a much higher body of water than at present.

0.85   13.15 **Sulphur Hills** are about 4 miles to the east across the Yellowstone River. The highest one has an elevation of 8,500 feet. **Ebro Springs** and **Vermilion Springs** at the south base of the hills are the two groups of hot springs in this area north of Pelican Creek. Beyond Sulphur Hills, at the headwaters of Pelican Creek, are several other thermal areas —**The Mushpots** and **The Mudkettles** being the names ap-

plied; in one group is a roaring steam vent. The valley of Pelican Creek is a year-round range of bison.

2.45   11.55 Camp sites east of the road.

2.90   11.10 Yellowstone River rapids.

4.60   9.40 **Elephant Back** (8,600 ft.) at the west was named in 1871 by Dr. F. V. Hayden because of the rounded form of its summit and almost vertical sides. The trees on this mountain and along the road are lodgepole pines, the most common tree in the park.

5.30   8.70 In the bed of the river ¼ mile east of the road are several gas vents discharging streams of bubbles upward through the water.

The **Rocky Mountain fringed gentian** (Gentiana elegans) was chosen in 1926 (unofficially) as the Yellowstone Park flower. (Formerly state flower of Wyoming, it was replaced by the "painted cup.") It occurs in profusion in moist places throughout the park, and in color it is deep blue—almost violet. Although very rare a few pure white ones have been found in Upper Geyser Basin. Its name is derived from Gentius, king of Illyria, who is credited with having first discovered its medicinal virtue.

Indian paintbrush (Castilleja), state flower of Wyoming (called "painted cup"), is widely distributed throughout the park and attracts considerable attention on account of its usual brilliant red to yellowish-red

MUD VOLCANO AND DRAGONS MOUTH

color; it occurs also in colors ranging from white to yellow and orange. This flower flourishes in shady sandy places, frequently in grassy patches where its brilliant color is in marked contrast to the green.

5.70   8.30 Scenic side road (to Mud Volcano, Dragons Mouth and other thermal features.) **Mud Geyser** west of junction erupts every few seconds to a maximum height of 12 feet. Hayden (1878) reported eruptions 18 to 40 feet high lasting 4½ to 30 minutes at 1 to 4½ hour intervals.

Gen O. O. Howard and his command camped (1877) nearby when pursuing the **Nez Perce Indians,** led by Chief Joseph. The Indians forded the river and traveled northward; but the pursuers stayed on the west side of the river as far as Baronett Bridge—following the Indians out of the park near the northeast entrance.

Mud Volcano, probably confused with the Mud Geyser was reputed to have erupted in times past to considerable height. Its crater partly filled with mud is violently agitated by escaping steam.

Dragons Mouth at the north is a pulsating, t h u m p i n g pool of clear hot water, agitated every few seconds by bursts of steam issuing from the throat of its gable-shaped crater in the hillside. The cavernous crater, with green coloring on the rock, and its flashing tongue of boiling water and steam, account for its appropriate name. Near by are several vents and muddy hot springs.

5.90   8.10 Northeast end of loop side road.

6.00   8.00 Below the stone wall may be seen several caldrons and steam vents between the road and the Yellowstone River. Chief among these is the **Sulphur Caldron** which contains large amounts of free sulphur in suspension, named (1937) by Superintendent Edmund B. Rogers.

6.20   7.80 About a hundred yards west of the road is a group of five small **Mud Pots,** which, when recently observed, were hurling small amounts of mud into the air.

6.30   7.70 The road crosses the south edge of **Hayden Valley,** named for Dr. Ferdinand Vandiveer Hayden (1829-1887), leader of the famous expeditions of 1871, 1872 and 1878 of the **U. S. Geological Survey** in the park. Reports of these three expeditions which treat of its geology, thermal springs and geysers, thermo-hydrology, mineralogy, topography, paleontology and zoology, with illustrations and maps, constitute source material of inestimable value to students of the park. This valley, once an arm of a vast prehistoric lake of which Yellowstone Lake is a remnant, has an area of about 50 square miles, and is traversed by the Yellowstone River and several tributaries. It is part of the summer range of big game animals and is a year-round range of bison.

7.40   6.60 **Elk Antler Creek** crossing, elevation 7,687 feet.

7.60   6.40 A trail leads westward to **Mary Mountain** (8,500 ft.), **Mary Lake,** and **Highland Hot Springs,** near the summit of the **Central Plateau,** 10 miles distant, thence down Nez Perce Creek to the north edge of Lower Geyser Basin.

7.65   6.35 The form of the ancient Chinese monad depicted with remarkable accuracy in the meandering of **Trout Creek** just west of the road, is used in the trade-mark of the Northern Pacific Railway.

7.90   6.10 Trout Creek crossing, elevation 7,685 feet.

8.40   5.60 At the north is the Washburn Range dominated by Mt. Washburn (10,317 ft.) the summit of which is the highest point reached by the road system of the park.

9.60   4.40 Parking area; view of Mt. Washburn at the north and the valley of the Yellowstone River, which in ancient times was submerged in the lake whose surface was at one time 160 feet higher than the present Yellowstone Lake.

10.25   3.75 **Sulphur Spring Creek** crossing.

10.50   3.50 **Sulphur Mountain** (7,800 ft.) and other summits of the group of low eminences called **Crater Hills** are seen at the south about 1½ miles away. The hot spring area of this group includes many small vents and hot springs, some depositing sulphur, and a large beautifully colored area of disintegrated rhyolite, several large turbulent hot springs, and **Sulphur Spring,** which erupts at such short intervals 5 to 6 feet high as to be almost a perpetual spouter. Its water is clear and deposits sulphur along the runways leading from the crater.

10.65   3.35 **Alum Creek** crossing. This is the creek thought to be strongly impreg-

JOSEPH,
CHIEF OF THE NEZ PERCE INDIANS

equally interesting tales, sometimes attributed to Jim Bridger.

11.20   2.80 North edge of Hayden Valley, elevation near road 7,687 feet. A trail leads southwest and at **Highland Hot Springs,** near Mary Mountain, joins the trail which leads west along Trout Creek at the south.

11.95   2.05 **Spurgin's Beaver Slide** is described by a sign near the road. Capt. W. F. Spurgin of General Howard's command built the first road to cross Yellowstone Park, which was used in that memorable pursuit of the Nez Perce Indians through the park in 1877. Capt. Hiram M. Chittenden, in his outstanding book entitled "The Yellowstone National Park" (1895) states that the flight and pursuit of the Nez Perce Indians extended over 1,500 miles. In not fewer than 15 engagements the whites lost 6 officers and 121 soldiers and citizens killed, and 13 officers and 127 soldiers and citizens wounded. A large number of the Indian losses could never be ascertained but their known loss was 151 killed, 88 wounded, and 489 captured. The capture was made by General Nelson A. Miles and his command in the Bear Paw Mountains, less than 30 miles from the Canadian boundary, in Montana Territory, on April 5, 1877. Some survivors surrendered and the rest escaped across the border. Chief Joseph and a few of his followers were sent to Fort Leavenworth, Kansas, where they remained until July, 1878, and were then transferred to Indian

nated with alum, which accounts for the many weird tales as to the effect of its waters when used to sprinkle the roads shortening the distance, and if forded by the wapiti shrinking their feet to the size of those of a pronghorn kid, and other

GRIZZLY BEAR FAMILY

Territory. Seven years later they were established on the Colville reservation in Washington.

12.75   1.25 **Otter Creek** crossing. About ¾ mile up this valley near the forks of the creek, on August 26, 1877, a party of 10 men from Helena had an encounter with the Nez Perce Indians, which led all the way to Mammoth where 2 members of the party were killed.

The **grizzly bear**, of which there are about 200 in the park, is rightfully the most respected of all the wild animals. It is deep brown in color with a grizzled or frosted appearance. The weight of the average boar, which is 8 to 9 feet in length, is 600 pounds; the mating season is in July; cubs, usually 1 or 2 but occasionally 3 or 4, are born in January while the sow is still in hibernation, the weight of a cub at birth being only 1 to 1½ pounds. The annual hibernation period of the bears is from the middle of October to the middle of April, or if the winters are mild, from the middle of November to the first of April. This time is spent sleeping in caves, hollow logs, sometimes under buildings, or in other places where protection from the elements is afforded. The cubs usually hibernate with their mother the first winter after their birth but leave her the following spring. One of the mortal enemies of a bear cub is its own father, who may kill and devour it if the mother relaxes her diligence in keeping cubs and father-bear apart. This cannibalistic trait is common to most carnivorous animals.

The aggressiveness of the grizzly is greatly over-rated; we now know him as a marvelously sagacious wild thing, crafty in hiding and loving concealment. Reports of unprovoked attacks on man are very difficult of proof, but his great strength and agility make him the most formidable of antagonists when aroused. He is not afraid of the scent of man but is extremely nervous and any sudden or unusual movement alarming him might cause him to strike or bite.

So numerous have been the bear bites and serious scratches suffered by park visitors feeding and photographing bears, that park regulations were recently amended to read: "The feeding, touching, teasing, or molesting of bears is prohibited."

Park officials who are concerned with public safety are fully aware of the danger involved when park visitors and wild, dangerous, unpredictable bears mingle. They have seen the tragic results much too often; and they do everything possible to insure the safety of the people, many of whom are oblivious to this elsewhere uncommon danger.

Although the adult grizzly is not a tree-climbing bear but uses its long claws in digging out small animals and roots, the cubs are able to, and do climb trees.

Bears are omnivorous and their food is chiefly wild berries, fruits, roots, grass, honey, insects, frogs, reptiles and the meat of other small animals.

13.10   0.90 Near the Yellowstone River is the gauging station.

UPPER FALLS

GRAND CANYON

13.25   0.75 **Chittenden Bridge,** a Melan arch 120 feet in length, spanning the Yellowstone River, was built in 1903 by, and named for, Capt. H. M. Chittenden of the Corps of Engineers, U. S. Army, who was in charge of the construction and maintenance of all of the roads and bridges in the park for several years. Thomas Richardson operated a ferry across the Yellowstone River at this point for several years prior to the bridging of the stream.

ARTIST POINT SPUR

A 1.60 mile scenic spur road across Chittenden Bridge leads to Canyon Lodge and Artist Point on the south rim of the Grand Canyon. Center of bridge (0.05 mi.); south of the road is the camp site used by the Cook-Folsom party in 1869 (0.15 mi.);

LOWER FALLS FROM
UNCLE TOMS TRAIL

parking area and view of the 109 foot Upper Falls of the Yellowstone River (0.50 mi.). **Canyon Lodge** (0.60 mi.) with a large group of furnished cabins is north of the road. Saddle horses are available here for trips with guides along the south rim of the canyon to Artist Point and Point Sublime (round trip 4 miles), and to Crater Hills and Sulphur Mountain (round trip 10 miles). Behind the lodge is the head of **Uncle Toms Trail,** first built by Thomas Richardson prior to 1903. It was originally a crude, dangerous route down the south wall of the Grand Canyon to the base of the 308 foot Lower Falls, the name still applying to the newly-constructed and safe combination stairway and path now in general use to both the brink and foot of the Lower

Falls. **Artist Point** parking area (1.60 mi.). In 1938 the former platform supported by a scaffold at Artist Point was replaced by natural rockwork, increasing both the safety and capacity of this famous view point, without marring the beauty of the canyon. (A new field exhibit explaining the gorge is located nearby). The view of the Grand Canyon of the Yellowstone and the Lower Falls of the Yellowstone River from Artist Point is preferred by most visitors. Although nearly a mile away the roar of the falls may be heard distinctly. Beyond Artist Point a trail ¾ mile long leads to **Point Sublime;** and in addition to roads built part of the way along both the north and south rims of the canyon, are footpaths from which many fascinating views of the falls and canyon may be had.

Geysers in the Grand Canyon, which are known to erupt, are three in number. **Tom Thumb Geyser,** near the base of the Lower Falls of the Yellowstone reached by Uncle Toms Trail, erupts from 2 to 6 feet high, at such short intervals as to be almost a perpetual spouter. Upstream from Artist Point on the same side of the gorge, about ¼ mile distant, and only a few yards above the river is an unnamed geyser which erupts at an angle toward the stream, throwing its steam-enveloped, spraying water column about 20 feet. During periods of activity which are more or less irregular, eruptions last-

GRAND CANYON AND LOWER FALLS FROM ARTIST POINT

ing 2 to 3 minutes occur every quarter hour. Another unnamed geyser in the gorge, is only 200 yards northeast of and on the downstream side of Artist Point. It is reported to erupt at intervals of about 9 days, 3 to 5 feet high for the extremely long durations of from 1 to 3 days.

The **Grand Canyon of the Yellowstone,** termed by geographers the Fourth Canyon of the Yellowstone, extends for 24 miles northeast and north to the mouth of the Lamar River, at the north edge of the Tower Fall area. The Third Canyon begins at the mouth of Blacktail Deer Creek and extends about 7 miles northwest to near the North Entrance of the park. The First and Second canyons are south of the Great Bend of the Yellowstone River near Livingston, Montana, between there and the North Entrance.

The name "Yellowstone" is the oldest of all the names in the park. No one knows how long ago it was first used by the Indians in one form or another, but from the records of the few early French inhabitants of the west, the use of their equivalent of the name "Yellowstone" is known to date back to pre-Revolutionary times.

It is the predominant yellow color of the gorge that is thought to have been responsible for the name of this river.

The beautiful colorings of this canyon, in which various shades of yellow to deep orange predominate, and streaks of blood-red to dark reddish-brown, as well as eroded pinnacles that seem to have been tarnished in nature's forge, present an outstanding spectacle that has been termed the most brilliantly colored landscape in existence. Its cliffs and slopes, composed of disintegrated rhyolite owe their colorings largely to the various oxides of iron. Alteration of the feldspars in volcanic rock produces a large amount of kaolin or clay, which is light in color and adapts itself readily to the exposition of all the tints of color from pale yellow to the deepest red, which minerals containing iron produce. In striking contrast to these colorful tints is the deep green of the trees, which not only border the canyon rims but find ledges and slopes upon which to subsist in the gorge itself. Near the stream and part way up the sides of the canyon and at places where cold springs occur, as well as in the spray-enveloped area near the falls, are deep-green mosses and other plants which harmonize with the green waters of the river and the colorful earth and rock. Where yellow or red pinnacles have broken down and strewn their fragments nearly to the water's edge, are sloping streaks of brilliant color. It is the action of hot water, and steam and other gases that has quickened the decomposition of this volcanic rock and painted its walls with brilliant pigments. Especially in the spring when snows are melting and in the summer after heavy rains, the canyon takes on its most gorgeous hues, and one of the forces of destruction is then evident in the many avalanches which occur. When the walls and slopes are dry the canyon presents a rather drab appearance in comparison to the brilliant, flashing colors seen when the sun strikes its walls after a heavy rain.

At many places wild animal trails are seen, tacking with many switchbacks on gentle grades that lead to the water's edge.

The canyon is from 800 to 1,-200 feet in depth, the deepest part being east of Mt. Washburn, where there has been little or no alteration of the rock by hot springs and steam vents. In this part of the canyon, and downstream from Artist Point, are seen the least altered walls which are clothed with trees and other vegetation to a much greater extent than between the Lower Falls and Point Sublime. There are only two places below the Lower Falls in this vicinity where it is safe for human beings to climb down the canyon to the river—by Uncle Toms Trail down the south wall and at the Seven Mile Hole, a fishing hole, where Sulphur Creek enters the river from the northwest, 7 miles east of the Canyon Hotel by trail. However, on both the north and south sides of the canyon, steps and paths permit access to the brink of the Lower

Falls where the canyon may be viewed. Only those who have stood at the brink of this tremendous waterfall, which is about twice the height of Niagara Falls can be fully impressed with the great height of this straight drop, which is comparable to a building 30 stories high. Chittenden states that the average amount of water dropping into this chasm every second is 1,200 cubic feet.

GRAND LOOP ROAD

13.50 0.50 Canyon bridge over a ravine. **Jay Creek.**

13.55 0.45 View of rapids above the Upper Falls.

13.70 0.30 Trail to platform and the **Upper Falls of the Yellowstone River** (109 foot drop). Parking area is a short distance north.

13.80 0.20 Parking area, picture shop, and trail leading to **Crystal Falls**—a drop of 129 feet in three stages in Cascade Creek, a tributary of Yellowstone River.

13.85 0.15 **Canyon Campground** at west—cafeteria, cabins, camp sites and **Amphitheater**—reached by a side road. Ranger station, east of road.

13.90 0.10 Filling station, store, and postal station.

14.00 0.00 **Canyon Junction,** elevation 7,734 feet. (Slow 10.9 mile service road leads west to Norris Junction. This road is hilly and crooked—25 miles per hour is maximum speed allowed. This is an old road used before The Grand Loop Road was completed via Dunraven Pass (elevation 8,860 ft.) to Tower Fall and Mammoth.)

Northeast on The Grand Loop Road is the area including the Canyon Hotel, and north rim of the Grand Canyon, the Lower Falls, Point Lookout, Moran Point, Grand View, Inspiration Point—from which The Grand Loop Road leads to Dunraven Pass, Mt. Washburn,

LOWER FALLS. 308 FEET HIGH

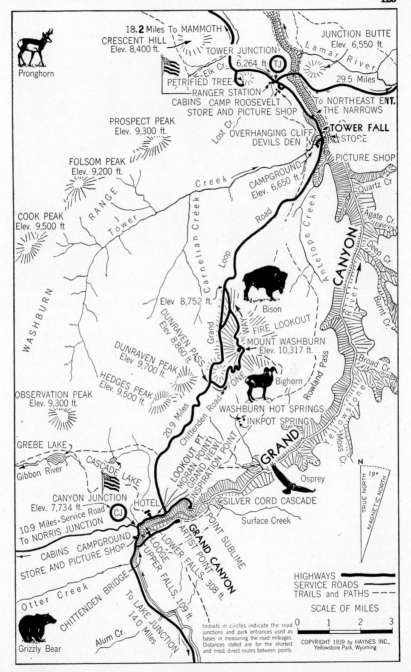

Pronghorn

18.2 Miles To MAMMOTH
CRESCENT HILL
Elev. 8,400 ft.

JUNCTION BUTTE
Elev. 6,550 ft.

Lamar River

TOWER JUNCTION
6,264 ft · TJ
29.5 Miles

Elk Cr.

PETRIFIED TREE
RANGER STATION
CABINS CAMP ROOSEVELT
STORE AND PICTURE SHOP

To NORTHEAST ENT.
THE NARROWS

TOWER FALL
STORE

Lost Cr. OVERHANGING CLIFF
DEVILS DEN

PICTURE SHOP

PROSPECT PEAK
Elev. 9,300 ft.

FOLSOM PEAK
Elev. 9,200 ft.

Creek

CAMPGROUND
Elev. 6,650 ft.

Quartz Cr.

RANGE

Tower

Road

Agate Cr.

COOK PEAK
Elev. 9,500 ft

Carnelian Creek

CANYON

Antelope Creek

Deep Cr.

Loop

Elev. 8,752 ft.

Bison

FIRE LOOKOUT

Grand

Burnt Cr.

WASHBURN

DUNRAVEN PASS
Elev. 8,860 ft

MOUNT WASHBURN
Elev. 10,317 ft.

Broad Cr.

DUNRAVEN PEAK
Elev. 9,700 ft.

WAY

Rowland Pass

Yellowstone River

HEDGES PEAK
Elev. 9,500 ft.

ONE

Bighorn

OBSERVATION PEAK
Elev. 9,300 ft.

20.9 Miles

WASHBURN HOT SPRINGS
INKPOT SPRING

GRAND

Moss Cr.

Chittenden Road

GREBE LAKE

CASCADE LAKE

LOOKOUT PT.
MORAN POINT
GRAND VIEW
INSPIRATION POINT

Gibbon River

Osprey

N
TRUE NORTH
19°
MAGNETIC NORTH

CANYON JUNCTION
Elev. 7,734 ft.
HOTEL · CJ

SILVER CORD CASCADE

Surface Creek

10.9 Miles·Service Road
To NORRIS JUNCTION

POINT SUBLIME

CABINS CAMPGROUND
STORE AND PICTURE SHOP

GRAND CANYON
ARTIST POINT

LOWER FALLS 308 ft.
LODGE
UPPER FALLS 109 ft

Otter Creek

CHITTENDEN BRIDGE

To LAKE JUNCTION
14.0 Miles

Alum Cr.

Grizzly Bear

HIGHWAYS
SERVICE ROADS
TRAILS and PATHS

SCALE OF MILES
0   1   2   3

Initials in circles indicate the road
junctions and park entrances used as
bases in measuring the road mileages.
Distances stated are for the shortest
and most direct routes between points.

COPYRIGHT 1939 by HAYNES INC.,
Yellowstone Park, Wyoming

LOWER FALLS AND GRAND CANYON FROM MORAN POINT

Tower Junction (where the Northeast Entrance Road joins The Grand Loop), and Mammoth (park headquarters).

GRAND CANYON
(north rim) and to
TOWER FALL AREA

High lights of the 20.9 mile trip to Tower Junction, are the north rim of the Grand Canyon, Dunraven Pass, the side loop road to the summit of Mt. Washburn (10,317 ft.) highest point attained by any part of the park road system, the incomparable Tower Fall, Tower Fall Campground, Overhanging Cliff, The Narrows (Grand Canyon), and Camp Roosevelt.

0.00   20.90   **Canyon Junction,** elevation 7,734 feet.

0.10   20.80   Camp site used by General Howard in 1877 while in pursuit of the fleeing Nez Perce Indians. **Cascade Creek** crossing above the 129 foot **Crystal Falls** in this creek.

0.50   20.40   Glimpse of the Upper Falls at south.

0.55   20.35   Start of **North Rim Trail.** Stairway (494 steps) leads down to the brink of the Lower Falls.

0.60   20.30   **Canyon Hotel,** ¼ mile north; elevation at this junction is 7,800 feet.

1.00   19.90   Path to **Lookout Point** and **Red Rock** west of the celebrated **Moran Point.** It was from this last-named point that the late **Thomas Moran,** dean of American landscape painters, who accompanied the Hayden expeditions on parts of their explorations in the 70's drew the sketches used by him in painting his masterpiece of the Grand Canyon now hanging in the Capitol in Washington for which Congress appropriated the sum of ten thousand dollars. Moran's paintings of important vistas and features of this and other Western scenic areas are outstanding works of art.

1.20   19.70 Parking area near rim of canyon.

1.35   19.55 **Grand V i e w**, one of the important jutting points from which thousands of photographs are taken.

1.50   19.40 **Grand V i e w Junction.** Near the n o r t h side of this spur road is **Glacial Boulder** (0.60 mi.) a granite relic of one of the tremendous glacial invasions of the park region. **Inspiration Point** (1.00 mi.) affords splendid, full panoramic vistas of the gorge in both directions, and the green water of the river threading its way nearly 800 feet below, but only a glimpse of part of the Lower Falls nearly two miles away. Across the gorge are Point Sublime and Artist Point.

(Note: Following mention of Artist Point on pages 119 to 122 in this text, are some general descriptions of the Grand Canyon.)

The **osprey** (fish hawk), a large, soaring bird, is commonly seen around most bodies of water in the park, along the 24 mile length of the Grand Canyon, and the smaller canyons, where it nests in the tops of

trees and on the summits of high rock pinnacles. Its nest is 3 to 5 feet across. The young, usually two or three in number, are hatched in June or early July and do not leave the nest for 40 to 50 days. They subsist largely on trout which the father catches and brings to the nest for the mother to break up and serve. The osprey, with its long, sharp, and curved talons and ample wing spread, is a capable fisher which usually has little difficulty in transporting its wriggling prey.

2.90   18.00 Service s i d e road from Canyon Hotel enters main road.

3.60   17.30 Along the road is a pure stand of **lodgepole pines**, which species constitutes about 80% of all the trees in the park. It is easily identified by its two-needle clusters. According to recent estimates, 85% of the park area is timbered.

5.10   15.80 The west bank, through which the road is cut, is a conglomeration of volcanic ash, obsidian and thermally-altered rhyolite.

5.80   15.10 The Grand Canyon, a huge gash in the wooded terrain, is seen from this point. **Washburn Hot Springs** on the southern base of Mt. Washburn, north of the canyon, are east of the road. In one of the groups is **Inkpot Spring** named for its inky water and black deposit of iron sulphide.

6.00   14.90 From here the distant summit of **Mt. Washburn** (10,317 ft.) is seen. It is a world-famous promontory from which, on clear days, the rugged terrain not only of the whole of Yellowstone Park is visible, but also many distant mountain ranges in all directions beyond its borders. **Henry Dana Washburn,** Surveyor General of the Territory of Montana, for whom this mountain was named, headed the **Expedition of 1870** which explored the present park area for the purpose of determining the truth or falsity of the countless stories pertaining to the wonders of the region, which though based on facts were rather generally disbelieved. Several other eminent civilians, a military escort under the command of Lieut. Gustavus C. Doane, and some civilian helpers comprised the personnel. The route lay from Helena to Fort Ellis, near Bozeman, Montana Territory, and across Trail Creek to the valley of the Yellowstone R i v e r, thence to the mouth of the Gardner River, near the present' North Entrance, and back of Mt. Everts by an Indian trail to Tower Fall. From this area the expedition moved south and General Washburn, who climbed the mountain which now bears his name, and the others of the party now began to awaken to the realization of the real significance of their explorations. They viewed the great gorge of the Yellowstone and its waterfalls, followed up the river to Yellowstone Lake and around its east shore almost to the southeast corner of the present park. From here their route lay to the northwest past the

Red Mountains to West Thumb Geyser Basin and by an extremely rugged and difficult course to Upper Geyser Basin, thence through this and the other geyser basins along the Firehole River to the junction of the Gibbon and Firehole rivers, where in their famous camp at the base of National Park Mountain, the national park idea was conceived. They followed down the Madison River and returned home. It was on this trip that Truman C. Everts was lost for 37 days and finally found. The important points which this expedition passed without seeing were Mammoth Hot Springs and Norris Geyser Basin. Due largely to the published reports and accounts by members of this expedition, serious attention was directed to the further exploration of the region, which altogether resulted in the establishment of the park on March 1, 1872.

6.30   14.60   Washburn Hot Springs thermal areas are in view at the east.

7.10   13.80   In the evenings throughout the summer it is not unusual to see moose from the road, on the slopes and usually near the bushy watercourses and timber.

Bighorns (mountain sheep) are found in the high mountain places where the scenery is grandest and where none but bold and reckless climbers would dare to go. The lambs are reared in the highest and most inaccessible places and, consequently, the larger birds are their only dangerous ene-

BIGHORNS ON MT. WASHBURN

mies. The bighorn is a gray-brown color; the average adult ram weighs 300 pounds; the mating season is in December; and the lambs are born in May and June—occasionally twins but usually only one. No other wild animal has spiral close-whorled horns, those of older rams making nearly a complete circle. The horns are very heavy and are circular in cross sections. The only animals in the park having true horns are the bison and bighorns, the pronghorn being the intermediate case. Male wapiti (elk), mule deer and moose have true antlers, which are grown and shed each year. There are 280 bighorns in the park according to a recent estimate.

7.30   13.60 **Junction** at **Dunraven Pass,** elevation 8,860 feet. This pass is in the southern portion of the Washburn Range, which separates the drainages of Cascade and Sulphur creeks at the south and Carnelian, Tower and Antelope creeks at the north.

MOUNT WASHBURN LOOP

The famous **Chittenden Road,** named for the government engineer who planned and executed it in 1905, ascends to the 10,317 foot summit of Mt. Washburn—the highest point attained by any of the park roads—from this junction, and descends and rejoins The Grand Loop Road on the north slope of the mountain. (Note: One should not attempt to take a trailer over this one-way side loop road to the summit. It has several sharp switchbacks and at places is steep and narrow.)

Starting up the mountain at Dunraven Pass on the one-way Chittenden Road (0.00 mi.), a view of the distant Grand Canyon (0.20 mi.), switchback (0.65 mi.), a view of the Absaroka Range (0.80 mi.), a view at the northeast of Electric Peak (1.40 mi.), switchback (1.48

LOOKOUT ON MT. WASHBURN   SOUTH FROM MT. WASHBURN

mi.), a distant view of the Teton Range at the south (1.50 mi.), switchback (1.72 mi.) from which, in the intermediate range at the west (from left to right) may be seen Cook, Folsom and Prospect peaks, switchback (2.10 mi.), whitebark pines and alpine spruce trees near the road (2.25 mi.), Dunraven Peak in right foreground (2.45 mi.), switchback (2.50 mi.), parking area at the saddle of the mountain (3.30 mi.), and via the left road to the fire lookout on the summit of Mt. Washburn at an elevation of 10,317 feet (3.62 mi.). (Rest rooms nearby.) Descending: Note wild animal trails used by the bighorns (3.85 mi.), saddle, turn left down the north slope of the mountain (3.99 mi.), Electric Peak in right distance ahead (4.10 mi.), canyons of Carnelian and Tower creeks, Cook, Folsom and Prospect peaks in intermediate range, and Electric Peak in distance—all at left— (4.90 mi.), Prospect Peak ahead (5.50 mi.), Electric Peak in left distance ahead at the left of

Folsom Peak (5.70 mi.), junction—the left side road is the 1.15 mile leg used by those returning to Canyon Junction, which is 10.75 miles southwest of this point (6.54 mi.), junction of the north leg with The Grand Loop Road (end of Chittenden Road) (7.85 mi.), is 8.60 miles from Tower Junction.

GRAND LOOP ROAD

(Note: Those who take the Chittenden Road over the summit may skip the next few paragraphs, and take up the continuation of The Grand Loop Road descriptions at the Junction, five miles north of Dunraven Pass).

7.40   13.50   Cold spring at side of road.

7.80   13.10   The mountains in the nearby range (left to right) are Cook Peak (9,500 ft.), Folsom Peak (9,200 ft.) named for the prospector-explorers who visited the region in 1869, and Prospect Peak (9,300 ft.).

8.60   12.30   The whitebark pines along the road are identified by the light-colored bark and their needles, which are in clusters of five.

9.20   11.70 **Carnelian Creek** west of and not visible from the road, is a southern tributary of Tower Creek. The deep canyons of both creeks are largely obscured from view by a dense evergreen forest. The bank by the road is breccia, of which Mt. Washburn is largely composed. This mountain is the summer range of a large number of bighorns whose trails lead clear to its summit. Wapiti and moose frequent the lower slopes.

9.60   11.30 **Junction.** Travel returning to Canyon from Mt. Washburn reenters The Grand Loop Road on this **south leg** of the road descending from the summit.

10.20   10.70 The mixed stand of trees here is composed of lodgepole and whitebark pines and alpine firs.

10.80   10.10 **Dunraven Peak** (9,700 ft.), southwest of the road, was named for the late Earl of Dunraven, whose Expedition of 1874 inspired his valuable story of the park, "The Great Divide" (1876). At the west Cook, Folsom, and Prospect peaks of the Washburn Range are again seen.

11.40   9.50 The forest-covered gash of the canyon of Tower Creek is seen again and closer, at the west.

12.20   8.70 The fragments in the breccia of Mt. Washburn are characteristic of explosive volcanic deposits, rather than fissure flows, which to a large extent are thought to be responsible for the rhyolite porphyry composing most of the park plateau.

12.30   8.60 **Junction,** elevation 8,752 feet, where the one-way **north leg** of the road descending from the summit, rejoins The Grand Loop Road.

12.50   8.40 Deposits of green volcanic ash are seen in the banks along the road. The slope south of the road in the valley of Antelope Creek at the east was selected as the most desirable ski run in the park in the spring due to its accessibility and variation in the lengths of the slopes.

At the northeast in the distance are the peaks of the Beartooth Range outside of the park, and the peaks at the north end of the Absaroka Range. The huge mountain hulk, notched at its west end, is **Cutoff Peak** (10,300 ft.) on the north boundary of the park, 6½ miles northwest of the Northeast Entrance.

13.10   7.80 Note the deposit of breccia—fragmental volcanic materials cemented together.

13.45   7.45 The forest on the north slope of the mountain at the headwaters of a tributary of Antelope Creek is a mixed stand of alpine fir and spruce, lodgepole and whitebark pines, and aspen trees.

13.70   7.20 For more than a mile the road follows along the west side of the valley of Antelope Creek.

Bison (buffaloes), one of the most stately species of hoofed animals in America, may be

BISON (BUFFALO) STAMPEDE

seen from The Grand Loop Road in several sections of the park, but in the northeastern corner are the majority of this species of which there are about 1090 all told, in the Yellowstone.

The force in immediate charge of the bison is quartered at the Lamar District Ranger Station in the Lamar Valley on the Northeast Entrance Road. In this vicinity bison may be seen only in the early spring and late fall and during the winter when this section of the park roads is kept open to motorists.

The average adult bull weighs 1,800 pounds; a record one weighing 2,800 pounds has been reported by the American Bison Society. The mating season is in August and September; calves, usually one and seldom twins, are born in April, May or June. In color bison are dark brown, and at a distance appear almost black.

The Indians had hunted them for centuries before the white man came, yet bison still roamed the prairies in countless thousands for hundreds of miles in all directions even as late as Civil War times. With the westward advance of civilization, practically all the bison were killed. One hunting party of 74 persons was responsible for killing 6,000. Thousands were slaughtered only for their tongues which epicures considered a great delicacy. Idaho Territory inaugurated protective measures in 1864; Wyoming enacted a ten years' closed season in 1890; in 1894 all hunting in the park was stopped and severe penalties were imposed for poaching.

Although native to the region, bison were represented in the park in 1902 by only a few individuals in scattered bands which practically no one saw. In that year, through a Congressional appropriation, twenty-one bison were purchased and brought to the park. In the entire world at that time there were less than 1,700 pure blood bison, but due to protective measures, in the 20 years which followed they increased to nearly 13,000.

14.10   6.80   At the southeast about 8 miles away are **Josephs Coat Springs**—a thermal area at the north edge of several groups of hot springs extending through an area southwest of Mirror Plateau to the drainage of Pelican Creek, 20 miles distant. On the west bank of Broad Creek, near Josephs Coat Springs, is the **Whistler Geyser,** which from a distance has been observed in action frequently. Although Cook and Folsom in 1869 visited this area, comparatively few others have done so due to its comparative inaccessibility.

Rowland Pass named for R. B. Rowland who with Supt. P. W. Norris and Adam Miller in 1878 explored this area, is on the eastern, low spur of Mt. Washburn. The swath through the timber marks the pass, high point on a primitive wagon trail long since abandoned.

16.30   4.60   Antelope Creek at the east.

17.75   3.15   At the west of the road is a basalt cliff. It will be remembered that basalt is the lava which was deposited in comparatively recent geological times.

TOWER FALL AREA

18.40   2.50   **Tower Fall parking area** (elevation 6,598 ft.), store (including delicatessen and lunch service), picture shop, rest rooms and footpath to Tower Fall.

Tower Fall, 132 feet in height, is in Tower Creek a short distance above its mouth. The pinnacles or towers which surround the brink of this fall are responsible for the name given it in 1870 by members of the expedition of that year. Footpaths lead from the parking area to the platform from which the fall is viewed, and on down the ridge where it forks, one branch going to the foot of the fall and the other to **Undercliff Springs** on the west bank of the Yellowstone River between the mouths of Antelope and Tower creeks. There is trout fishing in the Yellowstone River as well as in the two tributaries mentioned. Some fishermen go up the river a considerable distance, and although traveling is quite rough, good catches have been made.

Tower Fall Campground Junction. Spur road ½ mile southwest to **Campground, Amphitheater,** camp sites with running water, tables and rest rooms.

At the west of the campground the **Great Trail** of the Indians crossed Tower Creek. At the east at the **Bannock Ford** it crossed the Yellow-

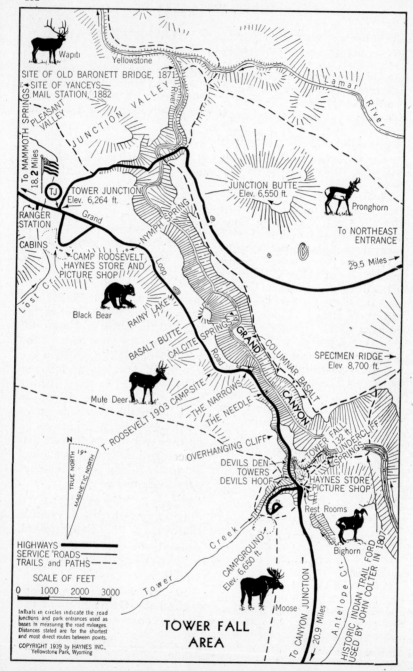

Wapiti

SITE OF OLD BARONETT BRIDGE, 1871
SITE OF YANCEYS
MAIL STATION, 1882

PLEASANT
VALLEY

Yellowstone

JUNCTION VALLEY

River

Lamar River

To MAMMOTH SPRINGS
18.2 Miles

TJ

TOWER JUNCTION
Elev. 6,264 ft.

Grand

NYMPH SPRING

JUNCTION BUTTE
Elev. 6,550 ft.

Pronghorn

RANGER
STATION

CABINS

Loop

To NORTHEAST
ENTRANCE

29.5 Miles

CAMP ROOSEVELT
HAYNES STORE AND
PICTURE SHOP

Black Bear

RAINY LAKE

Lost C'k

BASALT BUTTE

CALCITE SPRINGS

Road

GRAND

COLUMNAR BASALT

CANYON

SPECIMEN RIDGE
Elev. 8,700 ft.

Mule Deer

T. ROOSEVELT 1903 CAMPSITE

THE NARROWS

THE NEEDLE

TOWER FALL
132 ft.

UNDERCLIFF
SPRINGS

OVERHANGING CLIFF

DEVILS DEN
TOWERS
DEVILS HOOF

HAYNES STORE
PICTURE SHOP

Rest Rooms

N
TRUE NORTH
19°
MAGNETIC NORTH

Creek

Bighorn

HISTORIC INDIAN TRAIL FORD
USED BY JOHN COLTER IN 1807

CAMPGROUND
Elev. 6,650 ft.

To CANYON JUNCTION

20.9 Miles

Antelope C'k

Tower

Creek

Moose

HIGHWAYS
SERVICE ROADS
TRAILS and PATHS ----

SCALE OF FEET
0   1000   2000   3000

Initials in circles indicate the road
junctions and park entrances used as
bases in measuring the road mileages.
Distances stated are for the shortest
and most direct routes between points.

COPYRIGHT 1939 by HAYNES INC.,
Yellowstone Park, Wyoming

TOWER FALL
AREA

TOWER FALL, 132 FEET HIGH

seen the eroded pinnacle called **Devils Hoof,** of which an engraving appears in Nathaniel Pitt Langford's book entitled "The Discovery of Yellowstone Park-1870," a published diary of the Expedition of 1870. The group of towers through which Tower Creek winds before reaching the brink of the fall was named the **Devils Den** at the same time.

18.65   2.25   The imposing wall of the Grand Canyon opposite this point was the subject of a painting by Thomas Moran, who accompanied the Hayden Survey Expedition of 1871. He called it "Sulphur Mountain," a name no longer applied to this feature. Dr. C. M. Bauer, former Park Naturalist and an eminent geolo-

stone River. (This ford was used by John Colter in 1807.) The southerly trail of the Indians from Lake and Canyon joined the Great Trail at this campground.

18.45   2.45   Tower Creek crossing. Just north of the crossing, through the timber on the east side of Tower Creek is

OVERHANGING CLIFF, GRAND LOOP ROAD

EAST WALL OF THE GRAND CANYON NEAR TOWER FALL

gist describes this east wall of the Grand Canyon of the Yellowstone in detail. He states that, revealed in this cross section (top to bottom) are from 5 to 30 feet of glacial drift resting on lake deposits varying in thickness from 0 to 20 feet, basalt (columnar) 5 to 25 feet, stream gravels 110 feet, basalt (columnar) 5 to 35 feet and some stream gravels—all resting on a bed of breccia (volcanic). The pentagonal columns of basalt, which simulate a stockade in appearance, are caused by the cooling, shrinking, and cracking of the lava.

18.80   2.10   **Overhang i n g Cliff,** which rises above the road about 150 feet and slightly overhangs it, reveals near the road level a heavy layer of columnar basalt under a large bed of rhyolite. Close examination will reveal that these beds of lava rest upon river gravel and other stream deposits of finer texture which show even today the effect of baking resulting from contact with the molten lava. Parts of a fossil one-toed Pliocene horse were reported found in the gravel under the basalt on the west side of the Canyon near Tower Fall.

19.05   1.85 Below the highway, near the west wall of the canyon, is seen **The Needle,** a spire of volcanic breccia, 260 feet in height.

19.20　1.70　Parking area. A short path leads to a platform at **The Narrows** (narrowest part of all of the four canyons of the Yellowstone River) affording an awesome view of the gorge of the Yellowstone. At the north near the west shore of the river at the base of a large basalt-capped butte, is a thermal area known as **Calcite Springs.** Around the vents and springs in this group are deposits of gypsum as well as calcite. Some of the large masses of calcite (calcium carbonate) show concentric rings and fractures common to petrifactions of tree stumps. Characterizing this area are large beds of almost pure sulphur deposited by sublimation from the vents which exhale gases from deep-buried magmas.

In the fumaroles here, one finds well crystallized masses of sulphur mixed with bitumen of tarry appearance and odor—a unique occurrence in the park which seems best explained as a distillate from organic matter in buried sediments. (Hot Springs of the Yellowstone Park, pp 496, Allen and Day, 1935.)

(As there is no trail to Calcite Springs, the gorge steep and the trip dangerous, none but well-equipped mountain climbers should attempt to visit them.)

Magmatic gases of which about 98 per cent is steam, are believed to be the vehicle which conveys the heat from the central heat of the earth to produce geysers, hot springs, mud

GRAND CANYON NEAR TOWER FALL

pots and other thermal features on the earth's surface. Of the remaining two per cent most of which is carbon dioxide, only a very small percentage is the odorful hydrogen sulphide evident in the hot areas. In the Calcite Springs area—lowest elevation of any hot area in the park—Allen and Day found the highest percentage of hydrogen sulphide gas. (Carbon dioxide 93.2%, hydrogen s u l p h i d e 5.5%, other gases 1.3%.

19.30　1.60　This is the south end of a glacial spillway traversed by the road for about a mile.

19.35　1.55　Above this turn in the road is the site of the camp (1903) of President Theodore Roosevelt, who in company with John Burroughs, the eminent naturalist, c a m p e d through the park that year in the late fall. It was while on this visit that the President dedicated and laid the cornerstone for the arch at the North Entrance.

Winter snows drift in tremendous banks in the park, filling small canyons to their brims. The old-timers, who liked to impress upon visitors this phase of the mountainous country, found some listeners skeptical. Near the site of Theodore Roosevelt's c a m p (1903) near Tower Fall, the stage drivers called the attention of their passengers to the large head and antlers of an elk (wapiti) wedged in the fork of a tree 40 or 50 feet from the ground, and explained that the snow was that deep when the animal died, but they failed to mention, however, that someone had spent an afternoon placing it there in a very natural position as proof of the depth of the snow.

19.95   0.95   East of the road is small spring-fed **Rainy Lake**. The fringe of trees above it is on the west brink of the Grand Canyon.

20.40   0.50   North end of glacial spillway.

20.60   0.30   Junction. The loop road at the south goes to **Camp Roosevelt** (0.2 mi.) consisting of a main building, housing the dining room and office, a group of furnished and unfurnished cabins, store and picture shop.

20.80   0.10   Junction. Loop road at the south goes to **Camp Roosevelt**.

20.90   0.00   **Tower Junction,** elevation 6,264 feet. At this junction the 29.5 mile Northeast Entrance Road joins The Grand Loop Road. From here it is 18.2 miles to Mammoth, park headquarters.

NORTHEAST ENTRANCE

The most recently developed park entrance is the one at the northeast, near the towns of Cooke and Silver Gate, first made accessible by the opening in 1935 of a 69 mile approach road outside of the park, from **Red Lodge,** Montana, on a branch line of the Northern Pacific Railway. Bus service is operated between Red Lodge and the park during the tourist s e a s o n, making connections with the railway in Red Lodge, and transferring passengers to the buses of the Yellowstone Park Company for the park tour. **Beartooth Highway** ascends the tremendous south wall of Rock Creek Canyon in a seven-mile series of well-executed switchbacks and attains an elevation of 10,942 feet, from which it descends into the valley of Clarks Fork. Many interesting views are had of two outstanding landmarks, **Pilot Peak** (11,740 ft.) and **Index Peak** (11,500 ft.) located close together about 6 miles east of the park boundary. T h e s e peaks are most formidable spires, which until only recently successfully defied most experienced mountain climbers of the world. **Cooke,** Montana, 3.36 miles east of the park boundary on the approach road, was established as a mining town in 1870, two years prior to the establishment of the park, and until 1935, when the approach road was completed, the only route from Cooke to any railroad or main highway was through the park, and when the highways were closed by snow the mail for Cooke was transported on sleds, snowshoes and skis. It is said that a large amount of gold and silver ore has been produced in this vicinity. The whole area has been thoroughly prospected and the tunnels and rock dumps are in evidence even high up on many of the peaks. This town, which is beautifully situated in the shadow of **Republic Peak** (10,-086 ft.), has grown considerably both in population and business facilities since the completion of the approach road. To the north is the famous **Grasshopper Glacier** on Iceberg Peak, reached only by trail. It is here that myriads of grasshoppers have been impacted in the ice, which has preserved them for many years. The town of **Silver Gate**, Montana, about a mile east of the park boundary on the approach road, established within the last decade, has been built up largely to cater to the traveling public, and affords a variety of accommodations and business facilities.

NORTHEAST ENTRANCE
to
TOWER FALL AREA

This 29.5 mile entrance road from the park boundary to The Grand Loop Road of the Park at Tower Junction, f o l l o w s down **Soda Butte Creek** to its junction with the Lamar River, principal eastern tributary of the Yellowstone River, into which it flows in the Tower Fall area at the north end of the Grand Canyon of the Yellowstone. All along this route are seen the high mountain peaks at the north end of the Absaroka Range. This is an historic route, having been used by Indians, trappers, fur traders (including John Colter 1807), explorers, prospectors and miners, and was used by Gen. O. O. Howard's c o m m a n d (1877) when in pursuit of the Nez Perce Indians. About 11 miles east of Tower Junction is Specimen Ridge, where interesting specimens of petrifaction are revealed.

(NOTE: The first distance figure shown at the beginning of key paragraphs, applies to those traveling in the same direction as the sequence of paragraphs. Those traveling in the opposite direction, read the paragraphs in reverse order and use the second, instead of the first, distance figure.)

0.00   29.50   **Park boundary,** elevation 7,365 feet.

0.35   29.15   Rest rooms.

0.40   29.10   **Checking station.** Nearby are the ranger headquarters. **National Park Service** rangers at the checking station here as at all park entrances, record all vehicles entering and leaving the park and issue season permits, upon payment of the motor vehicle license fees prescribed by the Secretary of the Interior. Firearms are sealed. Dogs are per-

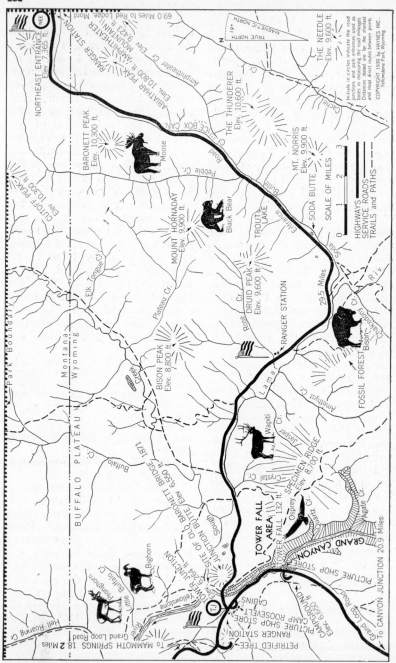

NEE

NORTHEAST ENTRANCE
Elev. 7,365 ft.

69.0 Miles to Red Lodge, Mont.

TRUE NORTH

MAGNETIC NORTH

Intake are circles indicate the road
junctions and park entrances used as
bases in measuring road mileages.
Distances stated are far the shortest
and most direct routes between points

COPYRIGHT 1939 by HAYNES INC.
Yellowstone Park, Wyoming

THE NEEDLE
Elev. 9,600 ft.

ABIATHAR PEAK
Elev. 10,800 ft.

AMPHITHEATER MOUNTAIN
Elev. 9,423 ft.

Amphitheater Cr.

Cache Cr.

THE THUNDERER
Elev. 10,600 ft.

Cr.LICE BOX CAN.

Road

Pebble Cr.

BARONETT PEAK
Elev. 10,300 ft.

Moose

MT. NORRIS
Elev. 9,900 ft.

CUTOFF PEAK
Elev. 10,300 ft.

MOUNT HORNADAY
Elev. 9,900 ft.

Black Bear

SODA BUTTE

SCALE OF MILES

0   1   2   3

HIGHWAYS
SERVICE ROADS
TRAILS and PATHS

Elk Tongue Cr.

TROUT
LAKE

Butte

Entrance

DRUID PEAK
Elev. 9,600 ft.

Soda Butte Cr.

Plateau Cr.

Rose Cr.

RANGER STATION

Park Boundary

Montana
Wyoming

BISON PEAK
Elev. 8,800 ft.

29.5 Miles

Creek

Lamar Riv.

Clarkestonion Cr.

Amethyst Cr.

Bison

FOSSIL FOREST

Buffalo Cr.

BUFFALO PLATEAU

BARONETT BRIDGE
Elev. 6,590 ft.

RIDGE 1871

SITE OF OLD

JUNCTION BUTTE

Slough

Jasper Cr.

Wapiti

SPECIMEN RIDGE
Elev. 8,700 ft.

Crystal Cr.

Bighorn

Pronghorn

Little Buffalo Cr.

Hell Roaring Cr.

Yellowstone River

LOWER JUNCTION
Elev. 6,264 ft.

Osprey

Quartz Cr.

Agate Cr.

TOWER FALL
AREA

TOWER FALL 132 ft.

GRAND CANYON

To MAMMOTH SPRINGS 18.2 Miles

Grand Loop Road

PETRIFIED TREE

TOWER JUNCTION
RANGER STATION
PICTURE SHOP STORE
CAMP ROOSEVELT
CABINS

PICTURE SHOP STORE
Elev. 6,630 ft.

TJ

TOWER FALL STORE

Grand Loop Road

To CANYON JUNCTION 20.9 Miles

mitted in the park but must be kept on leash or in crates. Upon leaving the park all visitors are requested to report the number of fish caught.

The Northeast Entrance may be reached via Northwest Airlines to Billings, thence via the Northern Pacific Railway to Red Lodge, and thence by bus.

Fish and Fishing. Fish in the waters along this route a r e principally cutthroat (redthroat, blackspotted, native) trout. No fishing licenses are required within the park, but are required in the three states adjoining the park.

2.70   26.80   **Montana-Wyoming State Line,** 45° north latitude crossing. In general this line parallels the north park boundary, which is a little more than two miles to the north.

3.30   26.20   S o d a B u t t e Creek crossing.

3.70   25.80   **Abiathar Peak** (10,800 ft.) is at the east.

4.30   25.20   **Baronett Peak** (10,300 ft.), named for Jack Baronett, one of the rescuers of Truman C. Everts (1870) and builder of the first bridge across the Yellowstone River (1871) is at the west.

5.70   23.80   Another good view of Baronett Peak at the west.

6.55   22.95   Sedimen t a r y rocks appear in the walls seen from the road.

7.00   22.50   S o d a B u t t e Creek crossing.

7.50   22.00   Another view of Baronett Peak at the north.

8.00   21.50   North end of **Ice Box Canyon,** through which

the road passes for a mile.

8.90   20.60   **The Thunderer** (10,600 ft.) is seen at the east.

9.00   20.50   South end of Ice Box Canyon.

9.85   19.65   Pebble C r e e k crossing. Abiathar Peak (10,-800 ft.) is at the northeast at left of **Amphitheater Mountain** (10,840 ft.), on the park boundary. The Thunderer (10,600) ft.) is at the east.

10.00   19.50   Campground on Pebble Creek at west.

10.10   19.40   **Mt. Hornaday** (9,900 ft.) at west was named (1938) for the late Dr. William T. Hornaday, former director of the N. Y. Zoological Gardens, who was influential in helping to preserve the bison from extinction.

11.70   17.80   **Mt. Norris** (9,-900 ft.), a high point in the mountain ridge in the east, was named for Philetus W. Norris, p a r k superintendent (1877-1882) for whom were also named a geyser basin and a pass.

12.50   17.00   **Druid Peak** (9,-600 ft.) predominates the west skyline.

13.30   16.20   **Soda B u t t e** (cone), near the east side of the road is the travertine mound of an almost extinct hot spring. In a semicircle, beginning at the west and extending northward around to the east, are: Druid Peak (9,600 ft.), Mt. Hornaday (9,900 ft.), Baronett Peak (10,-300 ft.), Abiathar Peak (10,800 ft.), Amphitheater Mountain (10,340 ft.), The T h u n d e r e r (10,600 ft.), and Mt. Norris (9,-900 ft.).

13.90   15.60   North of the road is Druid Peak (9,600 ft.).

15.70   13.80   South of and near the road is the confluence of Soda Butte Creek and the **Lamar River,** the latter draining the large area east of the Absaroka Range south of that point.   This river has several important tributaries including Cache Creek, South C a c h e Creek, Calfee Creek, Miller Creek, and the Little Lamar River, all flowing westward, and a number of small tributaries flowing east or n o r t h which drain the **Mirror Plateau.** On a small tributary of Cache Creek about 4 miles southeast of here, are **Wahb Springs** in **Death Gulch,** reached only by trail.   Gas from the vents in this small gulch is reputed to have caused the death by suffocation of many animals, but when visited by the writer the remains of no animals nor birds were found. **Hoodoo Peak** (10,-522 ft.) on the east park boundary, and **Hoodoo Basin** near it in the park, are 18 miles to the southeast at the head of the Lamar River, reached only by trail. This is the "Goblin Land" or "Hoodoos" mentioned by Supt. Norris in one of his reports.   It consists of an area of tall, massed eroded rock pinnacles, which reveal to those who let loose their imaginations a large variety of forms of humans and beasts.   One is a sixty-foot figure of an old woman with a shawl thrown over her head.   Photographs of these rock pinnacles taken in 1894 and 1924 are so strikingly simi-

GOBLIN LAND—HOODOO BASIN

lar as to be evidence that the processes of erosion here exemplified are extremely slow.

18.45   11.05   Rose C r e e k c r o s s i n g. **Saddle Mountain** (10,678 ft.) near the headwaters of the Lamar River is seen at a distance of 15 miles. **Specimen Ridge** (8,700 ft.) across Lamar Riv., at the south reveals petrified upright trees and stumps of 20 or 21 successive generations, according to Charles B. Read, Ph.D. (1940). No one can say how many eons of time are revealed in this most amazing natural exhibit.   Each layer represents not only the smothering of a previous generation of trees by volcanic ash and rock, but the formation of soil, its seeding, and the growth of huge sequoia trees as well as their subsequent burial in newer volcanic materials.   In no other place in the world, according to Dr. Ralph W. Chaney, paleobotanist of the

University of California at Berkeley, Cal., has been found such an extensive **Fossil Forest** exhibit, or one that is in any way comparable to this in the number of layers of tree petrifactions. This is mute evidence of volcanic activity in the park region occurring at widely separated intervals throughout an expanse of time so great that it is difficult for humans to realize the countless centuries involved in the geological processes responsible for the building of the park plateau. We do know, however, that in this vicinity there are many petrifactions and imprints of leaves of plants which do not grow today above an elevation of 3,000 feet, which is evidence that in the building of this mountain range, an uplifting measured by thousands of feet has b e e n brought about by the mass being forced upward from its previous relatively low level. It is believed that the most recent petrifactions in the park represent an era antedating the human race by about forty million years.

18.65   10.85 The **Lamar District Ranger Station** is the headquarters for the force in immediate charge of the bison. In this vicinity bison may be seen only in the winter, (this section of the park roads is kept open to motorists), and in early spring and late fall.

18.80   10.70 The valley of **Chalcedony Creek** is at the south across the river.

LAMAR RIVER

20.40   9.10 **Bison Peak** (8,-700 ft.) is 3 miles north of the road.

20.90   8.60 At a distance north of the road is seen a dark-colored outcropping of basalt.

21.40   8.10 East end of **Lamar Canyon.** Next 8 miles west were rebuilt in 1940-1.

22.60   6.90 West end of Lamar Canyon.

23.30   6.20 Druid Peak (9,-600 ft.) is seen at the east about 6 miles distant.

23.40   6.10 Junction of a spur side road leading north along **Slough Creek.** Valley of Slough Creek at north.

23.95   5.55 **Lamar R i v e r Bridge** (1941) 335 feet long, 38 feet above river.

26.40   3.10 **Cutoff P e a k** (10,300 ft.), near the northeast corner of the park, is seen at a distance of 15 miles.

26.70   2.80 At the south is the west end of Specimen Ridge

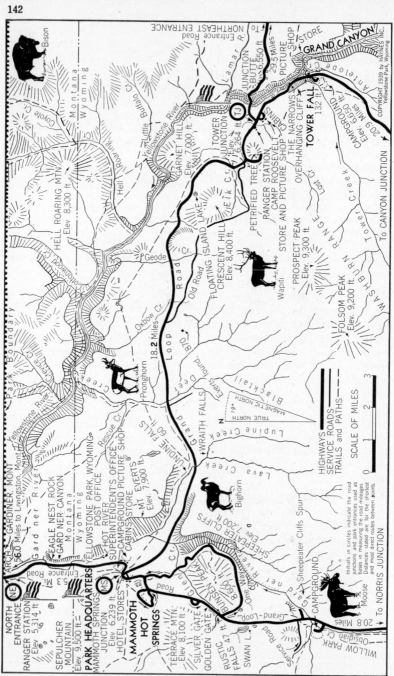

(8,700 ft.). This is part of the winter range of the bison. Petrifactions may be discerned with binoculars high up on the sides of the ridge. At the south 9 miles away may be seen the summit of Mt. Washburn (10,-317 ft.).

27.30   2.20   A glacial lake at north of road is one of three that may be seen in the half-mile stretch west of this point.

27.90   1.60   **Junction Butte** (6,550 ft.) north of road.

28.50   1.00   A trail leads north to the mouth of the Lamar River, where it enters the Yellowstone River, a short distance downstream from the site of the old **Baronett Bridge** across the Yellowstone, built by C. J. (Jack) Baronett in 1871. The old abutments are still in evidence.

28.70   0.80   Yellowstone River crossing, at north end of the Grand Canyon of the Yellowstone.

28.85   0.65   Grand Canyon of the Yellowstone at the south.

29.05   0.45   Cold spring suitable for drinking is at side of road.

29.20   0.30   Glacial moraine. Evidences of the transportation of boulders during the glacial period are all along the road at both east and west for many miles.

29.30   0.20   East edge of Pleasant Valley. Junction Butte (6,550 ft.) is the prominent knoll at the east.

29.50   0.00   **Tower Junction**, elevation 6,224 feet. The Northeast Entrance Road joins The

Grand Loop Road of the Park at this point. East of the junction at a short distance is the ranger station. At the south, reached by a short side road, is Camp Roosevelt, with a large dining room in the main building, groups of furnished and unfurnished cabins, and a Haynes store and picture shop.

Tower Fall (132 feet high) and the Haynes store and picture shop, rest rooms, and the campground are 2.5 miles to the southeast, near The Grand Loop Road leading to the Grand Canyon (20.9 miles) and Yellowstone Lake (34.9 miles). Mammoth is 18.2 miles west of Tower Junction on The Grand Loop Road.

TOWER JUNCTION
to
MAMMOTH HOT SPRINGS

High lights of the 18.2 mile route between Tower Junction and Mammoth (park headquarters), which in general parallels the north boundary of the park about 5 miles to the north, are the petrified tree, Garnet Hill, an interesting wild animal range, and a mountainous terrain of exceptional scientific and historical interest.

0.00   18.20   **Tower Junction**, elevation 6,264 feet.

0.10   18.10   **Lost Creek** crossing and ranger station. A short distance to the south is the interesting but seldom visited Lost Falls in the steep timber-covered canyon. At the north the nearby gentle slopes are fa-

PETRIFIED TREE

vorite skiing grounds for ama-
teurs. In this vicinity wapiti
and pronghorns are frequently
observed. At the northwest is
Pleasant Valley where **John
Yancey** in 1882 established a
mail station on the route from
Mammoth to the mining camp
at Cooke. In 1884 he established a hotel, which provided
accommodations for travelers
using the trail to Canyon.

1.20   17.00   An o n e-h a l f
mile spur road leads south to
the **Petrified Tree**, one of the
largest specimens in the entire
region. Its stump was partly
excavated and has been surrounded by an iron fence to
protect it from the fate which
befell a similar one situated a
short distance to the east, which
specimen gatherers leveled to
the ground, not realizing that
they were removing an object
of great interest, which future
travelers would have enjoyed
seeing. Millions of years ago

huge forests were buried under
showers of volcanic ash and
lava rock. "In the process of
petrifaction the cavities in the
minute tubular cells of the
wood become filled with silica.
A considerable percentage of
the organic material of the
wood, although usually somewhat altered and sometimes reduced to carbon, is found in
petrified wood." (Charles B.
Read, Ph. D., 1940).

By this process the structure
of the original wood, knots and
annular rings, is so well preserved that the species of each
tree may be easily determined.

Various salts in the perco-
lating water, chiefly those of
iron, account for the color of
the silica in petrifactions.

There are hundreds of petrified trees in the park, and innumerable prints of leaves and
twigs in this area.

1.35   16.85   Crossing   of
Yancey Creek. Glacial drift is
seen on both sides of the road.

1.50   16.70   Service road enters main road from the south
and continues northeast to the
site of Yancey's mail station
(now razed) in Pleasant Valley.

Columbine (Aquilegia), state
flower of Colorado, occurs in
several species, one of the most
striking carrying a yellow flower marked with red. They are
found in many sections of the
park in localities which are forested and rather high in elevation. The name is derived from
the Latin name for "dove" and
was applied because the flower
had a fancied resemblance to

a group of five pigeons. The Latin name "Aquilegia" given this plant (Latin "aquila" meaning eagle) is accounted for by the fact that the spurs of the flower somewhat resemble the talons of an eagle.

1.60 16.60 South of the road is a bank of volcanic tuff (impacted and cemented volcanic ash).

1.80 16.40 **Elk Creek** crossing.

2.00 16.20 Old b e a v e r dams are seen along Elk Creek at the east.

2.20 16.00 At the north is the furrowed face of **Garnet Hill** (7,000 ft.). This is an Archean, Pre-Cambrian, granitic gneiss, a billion years old. In the schists associated with the granitic gneiss are found small and imperfect garnets, which account for the name of this ancient hill.

2.35 15.85 Closer view of Garnet Hill at the north across the small canyon of Elk Creek, a southern tributary of Yellowstone River. The flat knoll at the east is Junction Butte (6,-550 ft.), one of the first-named landmarks in the park, originally called Square Butte. At the north of this butte is the junction of the Yellowstone and Lamar rivers.

2.90 15.30 At the south is the distant tip of Mt. Washburn (10,317 ft.) upon which may be seen a fire lookout station.

3.10 15.10 **Floating Island Lake** and **Crescent Hill** (8,400 ft. —composed mostly of an early acid breccia) are south of the road. Aspens which have been felled by beavers are seen around the south and west shores of this lake. Except in the immediate vicinity of the park highways, dead trees are allowed to remain; they furnish homes for many species of birds and when decayed add to the fertility of the forest soil. Just west of of this lake is a knoll of volcanic rock called trachyte.

3.40 14.80 **Hell Roaring Mountain** (8,300 ft.) is the cone-shaped mountain at the north.

3.60 14.60 Basalt, a comparatively recent volcanic rock, is seen on both sides of the road.

3.70 14.50 Garnet Hill (7,-000 ft.) is again in view at the east. As previously mentioned it is composed of Archean rock, representative of the oldest rock of the earth.

4.20 14.00 East edge of insect infestation of the trees. This is a case of Douglas firs being killed by the spruce bud worm, which feeds on the leaves and buds.

4.70 13.50 West edge of insect infestation.

5.00 13.20 Crescent H i l l (8,400 ft.) is seen at the southeast.

5.30 12.90 Hell Roaring Mountain (8,300 ft.) and valley of Hell Roaring Creek are beyond the Yellowstone River to the north. The grassy slopes in view at the southeast of the creek are important grazing grounds for the bison, wapiti, bighorns and pronghorns in the spring, fall, and part of the winter.

6.05   12.15 The aspen grove north of the road shows injury caused by the wapiti, which often feed upon the bark of aspen trees when the grass is covered with snow.

6.40   11.80 **Geode Creek** crossing. This creek flows northward to the Yellowstone River.

6.60   11.60 Beaver d a m s are at the south. The aspens and willows are natural food for the beavers, which migrate when the supply gives out.

The **rockrose** (pachylophus), belonging to the "evening primrose" family, is found in very dry soils and gravel banks at relatively low elevations, growing close to the ground. The season lasts usually until early July but a second crop of blooms sometimes appears after the first fall rains. The flowers are 2 to 3 inches across and have wide petals, which become pink or red as they mature.

7.05   11.15 The meandering of the creek seen at the south at the east end of **Phantom Lake**, forms an oxbow.

7.35   10.85 Beaver d a m south of road.

7.80   10.40 Canadian geese rear their young on Phantom Lake, south of the road.

7.90   10.30 **Oxbow Creek** crossing.

8.05   10.15 The cliff by the road is composed of tuff overlain by rhyolite.

8.30   9.90 Cliff by the road is rhyolite overlain by basalt. At the north is the valley of Oxbow Creek, a tributary of the Yellowstone River.

8.65   9.55 In the distance at the west is Electric Peak (11,-155 ft.). At the north are the distant mountain peaks (composed mostly of granite) of the Snowy Range outside of the park. Early prospectors traveling up the valley of the Yellowstone first discovered gold in Bear Gulch and Crevice Gulch, at the north and west of this point, which as well as Hell Roaring and Slough creeks they named.

9.90   8.30 Service r o a d from the east joins the main road here.

10.05   8.15 At the southwest is Bunsen Peak (8,000 ft.) in the foreground, and Electric Peak (11,155 ft.) at the west.

10.40   7.80 East edge of the valley of Blacktail Deer Creek. This valley is glacial topography.

10.90   7.30 At the north on the side of an unnamed butte is a deposit of red shale of the Triassic period.

11.30   6.90 **Blacktail Deer Creek** crossing. A service road enters the main road from the south. At the southwest is the Washburn Range, including Prospect, Folsom, and Cook peaks. Almost directly east of this point at a distance of slightly over two miles, just south of the eastern branch of Blacktail Deer Creek, is the grassy knoll upon the summit of which **Truman C. Everts,** who was lost from the Expedition of 1870 for 37 days, was found by Jack Baronett and George Pritchett. He was in a very critical condition, emaciated and out of his head, but in time recovered completely and although at an advanced age became a proud father after his harrowing experience. On this summit are the remains of a monument known as the Baronett-Everts Cairn. Two forks of the Great Trail of the Indians, known also as the Bannock Trail, passed this knoll on both sides and joined at the draw at its east.

Between here and Soda Butte is a great calving ground of the wapiti during their annual migration in May and June to their higher summer range. The cows leave the herd to rear their calves, until they are strong enough to follow.

11.70   6.50   Two limestone hills—rare in this volcanic area —one at the north and another at the east, are seen from this point.

11.80   6.40   **Lava Creek** formerly flowed through this valley to the Yellowstone River, when it was dammed by ice during the glacial period. It now flows northwest along the base of Mt. Everts.

12.00   6.20   The small lake below the road is the remains of a onetime large glacial lake.

12.10   6.10   Another good view of Bunsen Peak at the southwest.

12.70   5.50   Northwest of the road is an outcropping of rhyolite.

12.90   5.30   Northwest of the road is an outcropping of basalt.

13.00   5.20   Northwest of the road is an outcropping of rhyolite.

13.20   5.00   The valley of Lava Creek.

13.30   4.90   The ledge north of the road is rhyolite. The small valley at the north was formed when Lava Creek was temporarily diverted by a glacier, which dammed the main valley. The slopes in this vicinity are the winter range of big grazing animals and the summer range of pronghorns.

Pronghorns (antelope), of which there are about 600, usually in scattered bands, throughout the lower elevations in the park, are as picturesque as any of the wild animals in the region and the most fleet of foot. In color the pronghorn is reddish-tan with black and white markings. The weight of the a v e r a g e adult buck is 100 pounds; the mating season is September and October; kids, of which there are usually one or two, are born in May or June. This is the intermediate species between the horned and antlered animals, shedding the small bony sheath each year but retaining the horny core, but unlike the others, horns are common to both the buck and d o e. Both the young a n d grown-up pronghorns seem to follow shades, in their seasonal changes in color, which blend with the early and late colors of the vegetation, rendering them inconspicuous except to the practiced eye. They range in the open areas all along the road from the Tower Fall area to the North Entrance.

13.55   4.65   Southeast i s **Wraith Falls** in Lupine Creek.

13.70   4.50   **Lava Creek**
crossing.

13.75   4.45   Camp sites on
Lava Creek.

14.15   4.05   Parking area.
Undine Falls, 60 feet high, in
Lava Creek. The canyon walls
below this parking area are per-
pendicular and it is extremely
dangerous to attempt a descent
here except with long, strong
ropes. South of the road is the
east end of Sheepeater Cliffs,
favorite haunts of the nomadic
Sheepeater Indians who frequented this region. They were
a branch of the Shoshonean
tribe, small in stature, timid,
and with little worldly goods;
they had no horses, lived in
wickiups, and were armed only
with bows and arrows, and
clubs. Their principal source
of meat was the wild bighorns
which were plentiful in this
area.

14.40   3.80   Remains of an
old Indian trail, later used as a
wagon road, and now used only
by horsebackers, on the north
side of Lava Creek, are still in
evidence. The first road to the
diggings on Clarks Fork, near
Cooke, Montana Territory,
crossed the Gardner River near
its mouth in the vicinity of the
North Entrance, and ascended
the north slope of Mt. Everts,
back of which mountain it followed to Blacktail Deer Creek
along the Indian trail all the
way. The second road followed
the Gardner River and Lava
Creek to Undine Falls, much of
the way on the opposite side
from the present road. It is remarkable that **freighters**, driv-

ing 6 or 8 mules or horses with a
wagon, a trailer, and sometimes
a cook shack as well, could successfully negotiate those narrow, steep, primitive roads. It
was not unusual for the early
freighters to travel alone, handling the entire outfit unassist-
ed. In ascending the steep
grades the wagons were uncou-
pled and pulled up one at a time.
A snub block was u s u a l l y
dragged behind a rear wheel, so
that in making a long climb the
wagons would be kept from
backing when the mules or
horses took the tension off the
tugs and rested. The uncou-
pling procedure was repeated
in making steep descents, and
when the brakes could not hold
back the wagons, each was
rough-locked and driven down
separately. This rough-locking
was accomplished by chaining
or tying one or both of the rear
wheels so that they would slide
instead of turn. In some cases
trees were dragged.

14.90   3.30   C r o s s glacial
spillway.

15.20   3.00   **Mt. Everts** (7,-
900 ft.) is the huge, long cliff
at the north. On its face, on
and below the bench, is an 800
foot outcropping in which some
of the best fossils have been
found. The round boulders are
glacial and the outcropping under the cap of rhyolite is con-
glomerate. The main body of
the mountain is composed of
stratified marine deposits of the
Cretaceous period. The trees
are Douglas firs and lodgepole
pines. In the face of this mountain are numerous bear dens

where the black bears hibernate.

16.20   2.00 The mountains at the southeast and northwest (left to right) are **Bunsen Peak** (8,600 ft.), **Terrace Mountain** (8,100 ft.), **Clagett Butte** (8,100 ft.), and **Sepulcher Mountain** (9,500 ft.) ahead. On the lower slopes of Sepulcher Mountain is a large light-colored deposit of travertine and the hot springs, which are now active.

16.45   2.00 (Center) **Sheepeater Canyon Bridge**, completed fall 1939, largest bridge in Wyoming, is 805 feet long and 200 feet above the river.

16.50   1.70 The c a m e l's humps at the south is on a spur of **Sheepeater Cliffs.** T h e s e cliffs extend eastward for more than a mile to Undine Falls and southwest along the Gardner River about 4 miles. The Gardner River, between Bunsen Peak and Sheepeater Cliffs, traverses Sheepeater Canyon in which is Osprey Falls; they may be viewed from the east side of Bunsen Peak from a one-way loop side road which encircles the mountain, leaving T h e Grand Loop Road from the east end of Swan Lake Flat.

The vertical cliff capping **Mt. Everts** (at n o r t h) is parts of a lava flow from the magma which is responsible for the hot springs and geysers. The volcanic intrusions near the north end are andesite, which was intruded in a molten form and baked the sedimentary rock both above and below it. Near the base of the mountain, also at the north end, are seams of

coal and good fossil leaves. The big chunks of travertine, scattered throughout this valley by the glaciers, are from Terrace Mountain. The ice completely overrode the terraces at Mammoth and Mt. Everts and was probably nearly 4,000 feet in thickness. On the top of Mt. Everts are pieces of petrified wood and other rocks that were undoubtedly transported from the area of petrifactions many miles to the east. Glaciation played an important part in carving this valley in which in the old bedrock one can see typical glacial grooves.

17.20   1.00 Lowest point (elev. 5,997 ft.) on The Grand Loop Road.

17.85   0.35 **Hospital,** a n d junction of service road.

17.90   0.30 **Chapel** (a schedule of church services is posted in hotels, lodges, ranger stations, museums and c a m p-grounds).

17.92   0.28 **Amphitheater.**

17.98   0.02 Wye, Mammoth.

18.07   0.13 **Picture shop,** park headquarters of **Haynes Inc.,** south of the road. **Mammoth Springs Hotel** at west; government buildings including museum, post office, and superintendent's office at north.

18.20   0.00   **M a m m o t h Springs Junction,** elevation 6,-239 feet, where the North Entrance Road joins The Grand Loop Road of the Park.

(NOTE: Please turn to page 41 for the description of this area and continuation of The Grand Loop Road.)

TRAVEL TABLE
YELLOWSTONE NATIONAL PARK

The number of visitors during the period between the establishment of the park (1872) and the beginning of this compilation (1895), was estimated at not less than 1,000 nor more than 5,000 each year.

Year	Visitors	Year	Visitors
1895	5,438	1934	260,755
96	4,659	35	317,998
97	10,680	36	432,570
98	6,534	37	499,242
99	9,579	38	466,185
1900	8,928	39	486,936
01	10,769	1940	567,437
02	13,433	41	581,761
03	13,165	42	191,830
04	13,727	43	64,144
05	26,188	44	85,347
06	17,182	45	178,296
07	16,414	46	814,907
08	18,748		
09	32,545		
1910	19,575		
11	23,054		
12	22,970		
13	24,929		
14	20,250		
15	51,895		
16	35,849		
17	35,400		
18	21,275		
19	62,261		
1920	79,777		
21	81,651		
22	98,223		
23	138,352		
24	144,158		
25	154,282		
26	187,807		
27	200,825		
28	230,984		
29	260,697		
1930	227,901		
31	221,248		
32	157,624		
33	161,938		

TIDBITS of HISTORY

1803. Louisiana Purchase included most of the present park area.

1807-8. John Colter, former member of the Lewis and Clark Expedition of 1804-1806 and first white man reputed to have seen any of its wonders, traveled through the present park region.

1809. Andrew Henry constructed a fort near the outlet of a lake which bears his name, and is west of the park.

1827. The Niles "Register" of Oct. 6 quoted trapper Daniel T. Potts' letter of July 8 which described Yellowstone Lake and some thermal features of the park region.

1829. Joseph L. Meek, trapper and hunter, wandered into the region and later described Mammoth Hot Springs and other features, probably those of Norris Geyser Basin.

1830. James Bridger (1804-

JAMES BRIDGER (1804-1881)
NOTED FRONTIERSMAN

1881), trader, trapper and guide —a noted figure in the early history of the West—first saw the present park region. In November Joseph L. Meek saw and afterwards described Mammoth and some geysers, probably at Norris. (See Mrs. F. F. Victor "The River of the West" 1869, pp. 75).

1832. Antedated only by the name "Yellowstone" applicable in the park region is the name of free trapper Johnson Gardner who dealt at Fort Union with the American Fur Co., in 1832, and for whom Gardners Hole and Gardner River were named. (Chittenden 1927 pp. 94-5).

1834. Warren Angus Ferris (1810-1873), a civil engineer who visited the region in 1834, wrote the first account of its wonders which appeared in print. (See "Western Literary Messenger" of Buffalo, N. Y., issue of July 13, 1842; also Phillips edition of W. A. Ferris journal, Denver, 1940).

1835. Osborne Russell, a trapper, spent 17 days in Gardners Hole and a few days in Burnt Hole (on Firehole River) in 1835, and returned to the region in 1836 and 1839. (See "The Journal of a Trapper" by Osborne Russell.)

1837. Joseph L. Meek with a brigade of trappers under the command of James Bridger rendezvoused in what is now Hayden Valley in the park. A party of Shawnees and Delawares were with the trappers.

A Hudson's Bay trader named Ermatinger camped nearby, and a party of hunters with Captain Stuart, an Englishman. (See page 237, "The River of the West" by Frances F. Victor.)

1846. James Gemmell went on an Indian trading expedition with James Bridger in 1846 up the Green River to the Tetons, thence to Yellowstone Lake, Upper and Lower geyser basins, and Mammoth, thence down the Yellowstone River to Benson's Landing.

1851. Father Pierre-Jean De Smet, a Jesuit missionary, visited the park region as a missionary among the Indians in 1851.

1852. The first published account of James Bridger's descriptions of the marvelous features of the region were those told to Captain Gunnison on his Salt Lake Expedition of 1849-1850. (See "A History of Mormons or Latter Day Saints" (1852) by Captain J. W. Gunnison.)

1859-1860. Captain W. F. Raynold's expedition, including Dr. F. V. Hayden, James Bridger and others, attempted to explore the region but were blocked by snow-covered mountains.

1860-1868. C. J. Baronett, George Huston, and Bart Henderson prospected in the Tower Fall area near Antelope Creek, and the junction of the Yellowstone and Lamar Rivers.

H. Sprague and Frederick Bottler prospected from Henrys Lake to the junction of the Firehole River and Nez Perce Creek.

1863. Captain John Mullan mentioned the geysers and stated in his report to the government that he visited them. Captain W. W. DeLacy, heading a large party of prospectors from Montana, struck the Snake River near Henrys Fork and proceeded to Jackson Hole where the party disbanded. Accompanied by part of the party, Captain DeLacy followed up the Snake River and Lewis Fork and discovered both Lewis and Shoshone lakes, and Shoshone and Lower geyser basins. (See DeLacy's map of Montana Territory published by the Territory in 1864-1865 which shows the route.)

1869. Charles W. Cook, David E. Folsom, and William Peterson made a memorable prospecting trip through the park region in 1869, following up the Yellowstone River to Tower Fall where they forded the Yellowstone. They traveled up the Lamar River for about 9 miles thence southwest on the east side of the canyon to the falls of the Yellowstone, and around the west shore of Yellowstone Lake to West Thumb. From there they traveled to Shoshone Lake and thence northwest missing the Upper Geyser Basin but emerging from the forest at Lower Geyser Basin. They followed down the Firehole River to Madison Junction, and down the Madison River. (See the Chicago "Western Monthly" issue of July, 1870— story by Charles W. Cook and David E. Folsom.)

1870. The Expedition of 1870, headed by Surveyor Gen. H. D. Washburn, followed a route similar to that of the Expedition of 1869 as far as Tower Fall, thence on the west side of the Yellowstone River to the falls of the Yellowstone. The party traveled around Yellowstone Lake on its east and south sides to West Thumb and on to Upper, Midway, and Lower geyser basins and down the Firehole and Madison rivers.

1871. An U. S. Geological Survey expedition, headed by Dr. F. V. Hayden, began the first official governmental exploration and study of the region which the following year became Yellowstone National Park. William H. Jackson, a member of the expedition, took the first photographs and Thomas Moran, official artist, made the first paintings of the park. Captain J. W. Barlow and Captain D. P. Heap of the Corps of Engineers, U. S. Army, made explorations in the region this same year. Settlement began with the arrival of James C. McCartney and Matthew McGuirk, who built log cabins at Mammoth in Clematis Gulch and near Hot River, while C. J. (Jack) Baronett was building a bridge across the Yellowstone River just above the mouth of the Lamar River.

1872. On March 1, 1872, President Ulysses S. Grant signed the Act of Dedication establishing Yellowstone National Park. Nathaniel Pitt Langford, diarist of the Expedition of 1870, became the first superintendent. E. S. Topping and Dwight Woodruff discovered Norris Geyser Basin. The U. S. Geological Survey under Dr. F. V. Hayden continued work in the park, discovered Heart Lake Geyser Basin, and built the "Annie"—first boat on Yellowstone Lake—for purposes of exploration.

Travel in the park was by horses and pack trains, as wagon roads had not yet entered the region.

1873. Captain W. A. Jones with Professor Theo. Comstock and a large party traveled through the park. They discovered Togwotee Pass southeast of the reservation, and verified the trappers' legend of a two-ocean river (headwaters of Atlantic and Pacific creeks

NATHANIEL PITT LANGFORD
(1832-1911)
FIRST SUPERINTENDENT OF THE PARK (1872-1877)

south of Yellowstone's Two Ocean Plateau).

1874. The Scottish Earl of Dunraven made an extensive hunting trip through the region. His book "The Great Divide" (1876) is important in park literature. Another outstanding writer, Rev. E. I. Stanley, author of "Rambles in Wonderland," visited the park this same year.

1875. Captain William Ludlow, in charge of reconnaissance in central Montana Territory, made measurements of the falls of the Yellowstone. E. S. Topping, author of "Chronicles of the Yellowstone" (1888), built the "Topping," the second boat on Yellowstone Lake. The first list of park fauna by George Bird Grinnell was compiled, and the first park explorations by Philetus W. Norris were made this same year.

1877. Chief Joseph and several hundred other Nez Perce Indians were pursued through the park by General O. O. Howard and his command. "Howard's Trail" built by Captain W. F. Spurgin, was the first, primitive wagon road to cross the park.

General W. T. Sherman with an escort of five men visited the park.

1878. Supt. P. W. Norris built the Norris Road from Mammoth (through Snow Pass) to Norris and Lower geyser basins. Monument Geyser Basin was discovered. General Nelson A. Miles, captor of the Nez Perce Indians near the north boundary of Montana Territory,

toured the park. The U. S. Geological Survey, under the leadership of Dr. F. V. Hayden, resumed the task of exploration, study, and mapping, and recording the scientific and historical facts about the region and its features. (See "U. S. Geological Survey of Montana and Adjacent Territory 1871;" "U. S. Geological Survey of Montana, Idaho, Wyoming, and Utah 1872;" and "U. S. Geological and Geographical Survey of the Territories of Wyoming and Idaho 1878," Part I and Part II—all by F. V. Hayden— source books of inestimable value.)

Bannock Indians made a raid into the park and stole some horses.

1879. A park headquarters building was built by Supt. P. W. Norris on the summit of Capitol Hill (razed 1909). Norris also discovered and named Norris Pass. The first signs, denoting important features and distances, were installed. The first white men to spend the winter in the park—A. F. Norris, C. M. Stephens, and J. Davis—lived throughout the winter of 1879-1880 in the headquarters building at Mammoth.

Johnson, Manning and Yellowstone Kelly were Government scouts.

The park had 90 miles of travelable roads. Wagons and carriages were more in evidence than last year.

1880. T. Elwood "Billy" Hofer and his brother built "The Explorer," a small boat on Yellowstone Lake. Later he became president of the T. E. Hofer Boat Co., operating the boat concession on the lake.

The Marshall House, first hotel at Lower Geyser Basin was built near the confluence of the Firehole River and Nez Perce Creek by George W. Marshall and a man named Goff, who together also erected mail stations at Riverside, 4.1 mi. east of the West Entrance, and at Norris.

Mammoth Hot Springs post office in National Park County was established Mar. 2, 1880, with Clarence M. Stephen as postmaster. On Sept. 13, the Firehole, Wyo., post office at the Marshall House, with Sarah Marshall as postmistress, was established.

Harry Yount, the park's first game keeper, built a log cabin near Soda Butte.

1881. General Phil H. Sheridan and Senator Benjamin Harrison (Indiana) toured the park. Frank Jay Haynes drove a team to and through the park while Indians were still bad in the Yellowstone Valley, and the Northern Pacific Railroad had not yet reached Miles City, Montana Territory. On this, his first visit to the park, he took 119 stereoscopic photographs of park scenery and features at Mammoth, the geyser basins, (Norris, L o w e r, Midway and Upper), Yellowstone Lake, Mud V o l c a n o, Grand Canyon and Tower Fall.

He became the authorized park photographer in 1883.)

Primitive roads reached the geyser basins from the north and west park gates, and crossed Mary Mountain to the Yellowstone River in Hayden Valley—thence south to the outlet of Yellowstone Lake, and north to Alum Creek, south of the Upper Falls. From Alum Creek only a trail led to the Grand Canyon, Dunraven Pass and Tower Fall; but from Mammoth, a primitive road had been built as far east as Baronett Bridge, and south, above Overhanging Cliff, nearly to Tower Creek.

1882. John Yancey erected a small mail station in Pleasant Valley in the Tower Fall area. George Henderson, brother of Congressman D. B. Henderson (Iowa) was appointed assistant superintendent.

The Montana strip of the park was sold to the U. S. by the Crows (Absaroka) in 1880; ratified by Congress April 11, 1882.

Lillie Henderson was appointed postmistress at Mammoth July 5.

The Firehole, Wyo., post office was discontinued Dec. 5, 1882, and mail was ordered sent to Mammoth Hot Springs.

1883. The Northern Pacific Railway branch was completed to Cinnabar (3 miles west of Gardiner) Montana. The Yellowstone Park Improvement Company was organized; Mammoth Hotel was partly completed; tent hotels were operated at Lower and Upper geyser basins and at Grand Canyon (near Canyon Junction). Lieutenant Dan C. Kingman of the Corps of Engineers, U. S. Army, was in charge of road construction in the park. Dr. Arnold Hague and John H. Renshawe of the U. S. Geological Survey studied the park.

President Chester A. Arthur visited the park with a large party including Robert T. Lincoln, Secretary of War, Senator George Graham Vest, General Phil H. Sheridan, General Anson Stager, Colonel Michael V. Sheridan, Colonel J. F. Gregory, Captain Philo Clark, Governor Schuyler Crosby (Montana), Judge Rawlins, and Official Photographer Frank Jay Haynes.

Henry Villard, president of the Northern Pacific Railroad, and a party of distinguished persons of the "Villard Excursion," celebrating the completion of the railway (the last spike was driven near Gold Creek), visited the park. Frank Jay Haynes accompanied the excursion from Saint Paul to the coast as official photographer.

1884. C. T. Hobart built a hotel on the lease of the Yellowstone Park Improvement Company at Lower Geyser Basin, near the junction of Firehole River and Nez Perce Creek, the company having suffered financial difficulties. John F. Yancey secured a permit to erect a hotel on his site in Pleasant Valley. The first Haynes picture shop in the park was built in 1884 on the parade ground at Mammoth by Frank Jay Haynes. It was moved in 1903 to the foot of Capitol Hill, and was razed (1928) upon completion of the present headquarters building of Haynes Inc.

George W. Wakefield put on a line of Concord Coaches for operation in the park.

Jennie A. Henderson succeeded Lillie Henderson as postmistress at Mammoth, April 4, 1884; and the National Park County name was changed to National Park Reservation County, April 4, 1884.

1885. C. F. Hobart and Robert E. Carpenter built a frame hotel at Upper Geyser Basin on the present site of Old Faithful Inn (erected in 1904). The Cottage Hotel at Mammoth (now used as a dormitory for company employees) was built by Walter and Helen L. Henderson. The Firehole Hotel at Lower Geyser Basin was operated by George L. Henderson and Henry E. Klamer, his son-in-law. Frank Jay Haynes bought, equipped, and started operating a traveling photographic studio, known as the Haynes Palace Studio Car, over all the lines of the Northern Pacific Railroad.

1886. The Yellowstone Park Association acquired the leases of the then defunct Yellowstone Park Improvement Company, completed Mammoth Hotel, built a hotel at Norris, and also conducted tent hotels at Lower and Upper geyser basins and at Canyon.

The Firehole, Wyoming, post office was reestablished June 17, 1886, with John Clark as postmaster.

Mrs. Marion A. Baronett succeeded Jennie A. Henderson as postmistress at Mammoth, Oct. 25, 1886.

1887. The Yellowstone Park Association built a camp hotel at the outlet of Yellowstone Lake, and constructed a camp hotel at Norris to replace the Norris Hotel which burned on July 14. A winter tour was attempted in 1886-1887 by Lieutenant Frederick Schwatka of Arctic fame and a large party, which, however, broke up at Norris due to the extreme difficulties encountered. Frank Jay Haynes, photographer, Scout Ed Wilson, and two assistants pushed on and made a 29-day complete trip of nearly 200 miles to the other geyser basins, the canyon, Mount Washburn, Yanceys, and then to Mammoth. Temperatures ranged from 10° to 50° below zero. A blinding snowstorm overtook the party of four on Mt. Washburn and lasted four days during which time they wandered day and night without food, fire, or shelter, before reaching Yanceys. Although this trip nearly cost all four men their lives, they were successful in procuring a series of winter pictures, the first ever taken in the region.

1888. Excelsior Geyser, quiescent since 1882, again became active. Jack Ellis Haynes first season in the park.

Jennie H. Dewing succeeded Mrs. Marion A. Baronett as postmistress at Mammoth, Oct. 19, 1888.

1889. Ole A. Anderson was granted a franchise to conduct a store at Mammoth for the sale of bottles of natural park sands and coated specimens. The Yellowstone Lake Boat Company, headed by E. C. Waters, was organized to operate the boats on Yellowstone Lake.

Montana Territory, created in 1864 was admitted to statehood.

1890. Construction of Fort Yellowstone was begun. Haynes Guidebook of the park was first published. Construction of the first road from Yellowstone Lake to Cody was begun (opened for travel in 1903). Canyon Hotel was constructed; Lake Hotel was under construction.

Wyoming and Idaho were both admitted to statehood. Idaho Territory was organized in 1863; and Wyoming Territory, by an Act of Congress, was established as a territory in 1868.

1891. Fountain Hotel (0.5 mile north of Fountain Paint Pot) was built by the Yellowstone Park Association, and the two small hotels near the junction of the Firehole River and Nez Perce Creek were abandoned. Lieutenant Hiram Martin Chittenden, Corps of Engineers, U. S. Army, was assigned the task of construction and maintenance of the roads, bridges, and other improvements in the park. (He left April 2, 1893, but returned as major on March 25, 1899, and was in charge until March 31, 1906.) The road from Lone Star Geyser (near Upper Geyser Basin) to West Thumb was under construction.

The Firehole, Wyoming, post office was discontinued, for the second and last time, May 22, 1891.

1892. The beginning of the season marked the advent of the Yellowstone Park Transportation Company, of which Silas S. Huntley was superintendent. Former transporting, also by stagecoach, was done by companies operated by Chas. W. Hoffman, Frank Jay Haynes, and George W. Wakefield on short-term franchises. Harry Wilbour Child (1856-1931) was first associated with the park in 1892 when, in partnership with Silas S. Huntley and E. W. Bach, the Yellowstone Park Transportation Company was formed. Upon the death of S. S. Huntley in 1901, H. W. Child assumed the entire management of the companies operating the hotels, and the transportation of passengers entering at North Entrance, and in 1903 bought out the other owners.

The road from Upper Geyser Basin to West Thumb w a s opened; the War Department finished construction of F o r t Yellowstone; the camp hotel at Norris burned in May and was replaced by a lunch station under canvas.

1893. George Ash, as postmaster succeeded Mrs. Jennie H. Dewing, at Mammoth, Oct. 3, 1893.

1894. Hon. John W. Meldrum was appointed U. S. Commissioner—the first in any national park—which post he held continuously until June, 1935. He died at his home in Denver, Colorado, February 27, 1936, at the age of 92 years. Chester Alanson Lindsley came to the park in 1894, later receiving the appointment as assistant superintendent, which position he held during many administrations. On Oct. 16, 1916, he was detailed as acting superintendent, which position he held until June 28, 1919, after which time as assistant superintendent he served until May 21, 1922, when he became the park postmaster. He retired on June 30, 1935, and died in Livingston on November 24, 1938.

Early in March, 1894, a party was organized to visit the winter ranges to ascertain the number of bison and photograph them. It consisted of Captain George L. Scott, Lieutenant William W. Forsyth, Scout Felix Burgess, A. E. (Bobbie) Burns, Photographer Frank Jay Haynes, Sergeant Troike, and two other non-commissioned officers. They traveled on skis and carried their equipment and food in packs. The route was from Mammoth via Norris to Canyon, where another expedition consisting of the late Emerson Hough, eminent writer, and T. E. (Billie) Hofer joined them. The party proceeded to Lake through Hayden Valley, where 81 bison were counted, and camped about 12 miles up Pelican Creek. They discovered the cache of a poacher, consisting of a canvas tepee, sleeping bag, provisions, and a toboggan; 6 bison heads were suspended in a tree. A trace of fire in the tepee led them to believe that the poacher was in the vicinity; to capture him was the next move. As it had been snowing constantly all ski tracks leading from the camp were obliterated. Some 5 miles from the camp, however, they heard 5 or 6 rifle shots in rapid succession. Hastening through the timber to an opening they came directly upon the poacher, who had driven six of the bison into the deep snow and slaughtered them all. Fortunately it was snowing so hard that the approach of Scout Burgess was not noticed by either the poacher or his dog until the arrest was made. The poacher, Ed Howell, was taken to the Lake Hotel and from there to the guardhouse at Fort Yellowstone. In addition to the 12 bison that were killed by this poacher, a small herd of 7 was seen in the Pelican Creek country, making less than 100 then in the park. Wapiti were seen in great numbers in the foothills of Mt. Washburn, on Specimen Ridge, along the Lamar River, on Slough Creek, and the Yellowstone River to Mt. Everts. Small bands of bighorns, deer, and pronghorns were seen on Mt. Everts. The open water of the Yellowstone between the lake and falls was alive with ducks and swans. Red foxes and coyotes were numerous and an occasional black fox and footprints of mountain lions and bears were seen. The party in about 30 days traveled over 300 miles.

Congress passed the Act of May 7, 1894, to protect the birds and animals of the park, as a result of the reports made by these two expeditions, which included the pictures taken by Photographer Haynes.

1895. The first edition of Chittenden's book, "Yellowstone National Park," was published in 1895. It has been reprinted and revised many times, and is an outstanding book on the park. Beginning with 1895 accurate records of the number of visitors entering the park were kept.

On June 2d the first Pullman car arrived at Cinnabar, Mont., 3 miles from the North Entrance, which was the terminus of the Park Branch of the Northern Pacific Railroad.

1896. William W. Wylie was granted a franchise to conduct tourists through the park and house them in permanent camps. This business was taken over in 1898 by a company known as the Wylie Permanent Camping Company.

1897. Fort Yellowstone was enlarged to accommodate two troops instead of one; Camp Sheridan was abandoned. Henry E. Klamer secured a franchise for and erected a general store at Upper Geyser Basin. Frank Jay Haynes built a picture shop (razed 1935) on the flat west of Old Faithful Geyser.

The first travel began over the road constructed from West Thumb via South Gate to Jackson Lake.

1898. The Monida & Yellowstone Stage Co., organized by F. J. Haynes, began transporting passengers from Monida, Montana, to and through the park via the West Entrance; the name was later (1913) changed to the Yellowstone-Western Stage Company. Operations of this company terminated when the park was motorized (1917).

1900. A new Norris Hotel was completed and opened.

Jennie H. Ash succeeded George Ash, as postmistress at Mammoth, Feb. 19, 1900.

1902. The Northern Pacific Railway extended its line to Gardiner, Montana, from Cinnabar, its former branch line terminus 3 miles west of Gardiner, and constructed the Gardiner station. Leroy Hill was transferred from the Engineer's office, U. S. Army, in Saint Louis to the park as chief clerk in the government administrative office. He occupied several important positions during a long period of service in the park, including that of assistant superintendent (appointed in 1922) and disbursing clerk. He had retired at the time of his death in 1938.

The name of Mammoth Hot Springs post office in National Park Reservation County, was changed to Yellowstone Park in Yellowstone National Park County, January 30, 1902.

1903. The road from Cody, Wyoming, to the East Entrance, begun in 1890, was completed. The first rail passengers from Cody entered at the East Entrance in 1912. President Theodore Roosevelt and John Burroughs visited the park. The President dedicated the arch at the North Entrance. Old Faithful Inn and the weather bureau building were under construction; the superintendent's office and the Chittenden Bridge were completed.

John F. Yancey died May 7, at the age of 77 years.

1904. Old Faithful Inn was opened; Lake Hotel was enlarged. Trestle 410 feet long erected over Gardner River below Sheepeater Canyon by Chittenden. (Razed 1939 when replaced by an 805 foot bridge.) William Morse Nichols, who first came to the park in 1904 as Second Lieutenant (3rd U. S. Cavalry), resigned from the army in 1905, and in 1907 became secretary to H. W. Child. In 1923 he became assistant to President Child; and became president of the Yellowstone Park Transportation Co., Yellowstone Park Hotel Co., and the Yellowstone Park Boat Co., upon the death of Harry W. Child in 1931. The Yellowstone Park Company, representing a consolidation of the three companies mentioned as well as the Yellowstone Park Lodge and Camps Co., began operations June 6, 1936, with W. M. Nichols as president and Vernon M. Goodwin, former president of the lodge company, as vice president.

STEPHEN TYNG MATHER
FIRST DIRECTOR OF THE NATIONAL
PARK SERVICE (1917-1929)

1905. The road through Dunraven Pass, last link in The Grand Loop Road, and the Chittenden Road over the summit of Mt. Washburn were completed.

W. W. Wylie, of the Wylie Camping Co., who had been conducting parties through the park ever since about 1880, established the first permanent camp in 1896, sold out in 1905.

1906. Camp Roosevelt, near Tower Junction, was built by A. W. Miles of the Wylie Camping Co., which name was changed to Wylie Permanent Camping Co. (1906).

Alexander Lyall as postmaster succeeded postmistress Jennie H. Ash, at Yellowstone Park post office (Mammoth), Feb. 6, 1906.

1907. The Union Pacific System completed its rail line to the West Entrance of the park. The Yellowstone Lake Boat Co. (E. C. Waters, president) was succeeded by the Yellowstone Park Boat Co. (T. E. Hofer, president). The Yellowstone Park Hotel Co. succeeded the Yellowstone Park Association.

1908. The Park Curio Shop succeeded Ole A. Anderson at Mammoth. The military force in the park was increased to four troops of cavalry, and was later reduced to three troops.

1909. The stone buildings of Fort Yellowstone were completed.

1911. The general hospital building at Mammoth was built. Canyon Hotel was remodeled and enlarged. The Gallatin road connecting Bozeman with the West Entrance was completed.

1912. Rail passengers first came into the park via the East Entrance from Cody, Wyoming.

1913. The Yellowstone Park chapel at Mammoth was completed and dedicated. George Whittaker, former scout, acquired the Post Office Store at Mammoth from Lyall & Henderson and was appointed postmaster. The south wing was added to Old Faithful Inn. The north wing of Mammoth Hotel was built. The annex to the hospital at Mammoth was completed. The Shaw & Powell Camping Co. (Amos Shaw and John D. Powell) was granted a franchise to transport tourists through the park and provide permanent camps for housing them.

The Monida & Yellowstone Stage Company was reorganized, and its name changed to the Yellowstone-Western Stage Company.

1914. Henry J. Brothers received a franchise to construct and operate a swimming pool at Upper Geyser Basin. Henry E. Klamer, owner of the store at Upper Geyser Basin, died.

1915. Effective on August 1, and under certain restrictions, automobiles were first permitted in the park. Charles Ashworth Hamilton acquired the store at Upper Geyser Basin. The all-time season record of 20,151 tourists transported with horse-drawn vehicles through the park was set by the Yellowstone-Western Stage Co.

1916. On August 25, by an Act of Congress, the National Park Service was created. The War Department abandoned Fort Yellowstone and withdrew the troops, which were replaced by National Park Service rangers. The Cody-Sylvan Pass Motor Co. (F. J. Haynes, President) operated passenger automobiles between Cody, Wyoming, and Yellowstone Lake— the first motor line in the park.

1917. Stephen T. Mather, first Director of the National Park Service, was appointed May 16, 1917, and served until January 12, 1929, when he resigned due to failing health. The use of horse-drawn passenger vehicles was terminated with the motorization of the service via all entrances established by the Yellowstone Park Transportation Co., which supplanted all operations of companies operating horse-drawn passenger equipment. Housing operations, formerly conducted by the Wylie Permanent Camping Co. and Shaw & Powell Camping Co. were acquired by a newly-formed company known as the Yellowstone Park Camping Co., which in 1917 operated camps at Mammoth, Riverside, Upper Geyser Basin, Lake outlet, Canyon and Tower Junction.

Mammoth Camp was established in the Spring of 1917.

U. S. Army troops were returned to the park for protection purposes. The military took over none of the administrative duties, however, nor was the commanding officer (as formerly) appointed acting superintendent.

George Whittaker succeeded postmaster Alexander Lyall, at Yellowstone Park post office (Mammoth), July 21, 1917.

1918. U. S. Army troops, returned to the park in 1917 for protection purposes, were removed, that responsibility being restored to the National Park Service. Army engineers were removed July 1. All hotels and several permanent camps remained closed all season on account of the lack of demand for accommodations due to the war. Permanent camps at Mammoth, Upper Geyser Basin, and Canyon were operated.

1919. Horace M. Albright became superintendent June 28, 1919, and served in that capacity until January 12, 1929, when he became Director of the National Park Service, which office he held until he resigned in August, 1933, to become vice president of the U. S. Potash Co. Riverside Camp, and Lake and Mammoth hotels were not opened.

Y. P. Camping Co. name changed to Y. P. Camps Co., (owned by Walter White, Roe Emery, Howard H. Hays and E. H. Moorman since May, 1919.)

1920. James McBride became the park's first chief ranger. The office of park naturalist was created and Milton P. Skinner was appointed to that office. William C. Gregg conducted his first explorations in the Cascade Corner of the park in the Bechler River country between Pitchstone Plateau and Falls River basin.

1921. Frank Jay Haynes (1853-1921) died on March 10. In 1920 he had completed 40 consecutive summers in the park, during which period he conducted picture shops and transportation lines, and photographed and explored the region. The opening of the south approach road was celebrated at Togwotee Pass. A party headed by William C. Gregg, and including Col. C. H. Birdseye of the U. S. Geological Survey visited the Cascade Corner of the park. The map was revised and many photographs were taken by Jack E. Haynes.

The stone lookout on Mt. Washburn was built.

1922. The semicentennial of the establishment of the park was celebrated with elaborate ceremonies conducted near the site of the camp of the Expedition of 1870 at the foot of National Park Mountain at Madison Junction. Samuel Tilden Woodring succeeded James McBride as chief ranger. Joseph Joffe, assistant to the superintendent, came to the park as a clerk on May 1. The Semi-Centennial Geyser broke out on August 14.

Chester A. Lindsley succeeded postmaster George Whittaker, at Yellowstone Park post office (Mammoth), April 25, 1922.

1923. President Warren G. Harding and Mrs. Harding and a large party toured the park. The Howard Eaton Trail, named for a famous Western horseman and guide who conducted more than a hundred parties through the park, was dedicated on July 19 with fitting ceremonies conducted at one of Howard Eaton's favorite camp sites near the southwest end of Sheepeater Cliffs. Frank E. A. Thone, Ph.D., became acting park naturalist upon resignation of Milton P. Skinner.

The large Mammoth Lodge begun in 1922 was completed.

1924. Edmund J. Sawyer was appointed park naturalist. Prior to boundary changes (1929) Supt. H. M. Albright, S. T. Woodring, Ed. Bruce and J. E. Haynes traversed and photographed the mountainous region from Death Gulch to Hoodoo Basin and Jones Pass. (Six-day packtrain trip.)

To study hydro thermal and topographic features around Yellowstone Lake, and its wild-life, and take photographs, a six-day shoreline boat trip in September was made by Park Naturalist E. J. Sawyer, Jack E. Haynes, and George A. Larkin.

The Wylie Permanent Camping Co., and the Yellowstone Park Camps Co., were merged into the newly-formed Yellowstone Park Lodge and Camps Co. Vernon Goodwin, who in 1924 had bought into the operation, became its president.

1925. Hermon C. Bumpus Ph. D., with Herbert Maier and Jack E. Haynes (Acting director of museums and ranger naturalists), made a study of the park and its museum needs.

1926. The Geophysical Laboratory (Arthur L. Day Ph. D., director) of the Carnegie Institution of Washington, D. C., in 1926 began an exhaustive study of the thermal features of the park. This involved devoting several summers to the field work in cooperation with the National Park Service, and a considerable amount of work the year round in the laboratory during the entire period. The results of this systematic study, covering all the thermal areas of the region, were published in 1935 in book form by the Carnegie Institution. This monumental treatise contains many references to earlier investigations as well as a huge fund of valuable source material resulting from the study made by the authors and other eminent scientists of the Geophysical Laboratory. (See "Hot Springs of the Yellowstone National Park" by Eugene T. Allen and Arthur L. Day (1935).)

1927. The formal opening of the Gallatin Gateway Inn on the approach road from Bozeman, Montana, to the West Entrance, was celebrated with elaborate ceremonies conducted at Gallatin Gateway Inn on June 17. The north wing of Old Faithful Inn was built; Fountain and Norris hotels were razed, having been closed shortly after park transportation was motorized.

President Calvin Coolidge, Mrs. Coolidge, and John, their son, with a large party toured the park August 22-27. Herbert Hoover, Secretary of Commerce, visited the park. Joseph Joffe, who had been in the superintendent's office in the park since 1922, was appointed assistant to the superintendent.

1928. Dorr G. Yeager apappointed park naturalist relieving J. E. Haynes as director of museums and ranger naturalists. Imperial Geyser first observed in eruption July 10. S. T. Woodring built the House of Horns near Mammoth Museum. The Laura Spelman Rockefeller Foundation made donation for the American Assoc. of Museums to develop museums in the park. Under direction of Hermon C. Bumpus Ph. D., executive secretary of that association, museums were erected in ensuing seasons at Norris Geyser Basin, Madison Junction, Upper Geyser Basin, and Fishing Bridge Campground, and several roadside exhibits were built. This program was started in 1928 when construction of the museum at Upper Geyser Basin was begun. The stretch of road through Firehole Canyon was completed. Cecil A. Lord, who was assistant resident engineer in the park since May 23, 1926, became resident engineer.

1929. Horace Marden Albright became Director of the National Park Service on January 12, and was succeeded as superintendent by Roger W. Toll on February 1. George F. Baggley was appointed chief ranger June 22. Boundary changes were made to include the Hoodoo Basin at the east, and the petrifactions at the northwest corner of the park.

1930. The Gregg Fork of the Bechler River was named for William C. Gregg, who explored the Cascade Corner.

Stephen Tyng Mather (July 4, 1867—Jan. 22, 1930), former Director of the National Park Service (1917 to 1929), who had resigned due to ill health, died.

1932. A winter wild animal grazing area (7,600 acres) was added to the park near the North Entrance. Clyde Max Bauer Ph. D., became park naturalist, succeeding Alfred H. Povah, resigned.

The Stephen Tyng Mather bronze plaque near Madison Museum was dedicated July 4, 1932.

1933. The Yellowstone Library and Museum Association was formed on January 26. Arno B. Cammerer became Director of the National Park Service.

1934. Postmaster General James A. Farley sold in the park, the first sheet of the Old Faithful Geyser five-cent postage stamps showing the reproduction of the famous geyser picture taken by F. J. Haynes. John William Emmert became assistant superintendent. The widening of the Golden Gate road and viaduct, begun in 1933, was completed.

Construction of a large wing of Canyon hotel begun in 1930 was completed in 1934.

1935. T. Paul Wilcox succeeded John W. Meldrum as U. S. Commissioner in the park July 1. The approach road from Red Lodge, Montana, to the Northeast Entrance was opened to travel. The first regular air service to any park entrance was established (West Yellowstone).

Claude W. Anthony succeeded postmaster Chester A. Lindsley at Yellowstone Park post office (Mammoth), June 30, 1935.

1936. First park telephone directory was issued. Roger Wolcott Toll, superintendent of the park, was killed in an automobile accident in New Mexico while on duty connected with the inspection department of the National Park Service. During the period from 1919 to 1929 he was superintendent of Mt. Rainier National Park two years, of Rocky Mountain National Park eight years, and he became superintendent of Yellowstone National Park February 1, 1929. Edmund B. Rogers, appointed superintendent of the Yellowstone on May 25, 1936, was at that time superintendent of Rocky Mountain National Park. The first regularly scheduled airplane flights over the park were established.

The Yellowstone Park Co. of which W. M. Nichols became president, and Vernon Goodwin vice-president, with Mrs. Harry W. Child principal stockholder, was formed in 1936 by the consolidation of all the "Child interests" in the Park, including the Yellowstone Park Transportation Co., the Yellowstone Park Hotel Co., the Yellowstone Park Lodge and Camps Co. and the Yellowstone Park Boat Co.

1937. "The Story of Yellowstone Geysers" by Park Naturalist Clyde Max Bauer, was first published. On May 30 Superintendent Edmund B. Rogers and other park officials made the first broadcast from an airplane over the park —a national coast-to-coast hookup. In midseason the new Fishing Bridge was completed. By the end of the season the new Old Faithful-West Thumb Road was practically completed, eliminating the last one-way section of The Grand Loop Road of the Park. Mammoth Hotel, having been razed in 1936 (excepting the large wing), was replaced in 1937 by new structures called

Mammoth Springs Hotel, which development included a large group of cottages. Rail passengers first entered the park via the Northeast Entrance.

President Franklin Delano Roosevelt and Mrs. Roosevelt with a large party made a two-day tour of the park (Sept. 25-26), accompanied by Superintendent Rogers. In connection with this visit the first park radio program from the ground over a national coast-to-coast hookup was broadcast from Mammoth, September 25.

1938. The new Old Faithful-West Thumb Road was completed. Mammoth S p r i n g s Junction and the Mammoth section of the North Entrance Road were relocated. The flagpole was moved to the new junction at Mammoth. Francis D. La Noue became chief ranger, March 1. Chester A. Lindsley died in Livingston on Nov. 24.

1939. All park roads opened by mid-May. Crown Prince Olav and Crown Princess Martha of Norway visited the park. Orren Joseph Douglas former chief buffalo keeper (retired) died May 25. Samuel Tilden Woodring died in Butte Oct. 13. Yellowstone Park Library and Museum Assn. published Yellowstone Fishes (book) by James R. Simon. The 805 foot Sheepeater Canyon Bridge was completed in November.

1940. Daniel Wallace Greenburg died in Cheyenne Jan. 2. Park open to motorists May 1. Goodwill tour sponsored by the Tri-State Yellowstone P a r k Civic Assn. culminated May 5

in ceremonies at Old Faithful. Gov. Nels H. Smith (Wyo.) and Gov. C. A. Bottolfsen (Ida.) spoke. Bobcat band (Bozeman) and the Highschool band (Ennis) played. Lookout on Mt. Washburn begun in 1939 completed. Lake Hotel and Mammoth Lodge not opened.

Newton B. Drury of San Francisco, Cal., became Director of the National Park Service August 20, vice Arno B. Cammerer who resigned and became Director of Region One.

1941. All concessioners' facilities excepting Lake Hotel and Mammoth Lodge were operated.

Joseph D. Kurtz became acting postmaster Mar. 1, and postmaster at Yellowstone Park, Wyo., post office Sept. 10.

Arno B. Cammerer former director of the National Park Service died in Washington, D. C., April 30.

U. S. Weather Bureau at Mammoth was abandoned.

Air attack by Japanese on Pearl Harbor, Hawaii, Dec. 7 precipitated U. S. into World War II.

1942. Mammoth Springs Hotel, Old Faithful Inn, Canyon Hotel, and tourist cabins and cafeterias at Old Faithful and Fishing Bridge and some general stores and picture shops were operated.

Cecil A. Lord, resident engineer died Jan. 1. James McBride first Y. N. P. chief ranger (1920), died May 3. Wm. H. Jackson who first photographed

in the park in 1871, died June 30 at age of 99 years.

Katherine R. Heavey appointed military acting postmaster Dec. 8, 1942, married D. Chew May 30, 1943, and served until Nov. 14, 1945.

Mrs. Mary C. Lambert, asst. postmaster was in charge from Aug. 16 to Dec. 7, 1942.

1943. Tourist Cabins at Old Faithful and Fishing Bridge some general stores and picture shops were operated.

Dr. Alfred M. Lueck became a partner of Dr. G. A. Windsor in the Y. P. Medical service.

Maynard Barrows was acting chief ranger from May 8 to Dec. 4, and became chief ranger May 12, when F. D. LaNoue began military furlough.

Fred T. Johnston became assistant superintendent May 18, succeeding J. W. Emmert who became supt. of Hot Springs National Park April 14.

1944. Concessioners operated substantially the same facilities as last year.

The first recorded eruption of Morning Glory Pool was about 6:30 PM June 10. Since then no other eruptions have been noted.

1945. Tourist cabins and cafeterias at Old Faithful and Fishing Bridge, and some general stores and picture shops were operated.

Alfred A. Bowman became acting postmaster succeeding Mrs. D. Orion Chew Nov. 15.

1946. Mammoth Springs, Old Faithful and Canyon hotels, Old Faithful, Lake and Canyon lodges, Mammoth Tourist Cabins, and both tourist cabins and cafeterias at Old Faithful, West Thumb, Fishing Bridge and Canyon, general stores and picture shops were operated.

Postmaster Joe D. Kurtz assumed office Feb. 6, upon his return to civil life, succeeding Alfred A. Bowman.

Dr. John A. Pearson assisted in the operation of the Y. P. Medical Service.

Clyde Max Bauer, Ph.D., became Geologist of the National Park Service, Chicago, and was succeeded Nov. 17, as Chief Park Naturalist in the park by David deL. Condon.

1947. Concessioners' operations were completely resumed as in the pre-war year of 1941.

George A. Windsor, M.D., Alfred M. Lueck, M.D., F.A.C.S., and John A. Pearson, M.D., as partners operated the Y. P. Medical Service, a branch of the Park Hospital, Livingston, Montana.

The year 1947 marks the 75th Anniversary of the establishment (1872), of Yellowstone National Park by Act of the Congress of the United States. In this anniversary year it is fitting to mention some figures to show the park's growth in popularity.

Nearly 8 million persons, many from foreign lands, have visited the park since its establishment March 1, 1872, when President Ulysses S. Grant signed the Act of Dedication. (See Travel Table page 150.) Records of travel prior to 1895 were meager; but were carefully recorded since that year.

The greatest travel year was 1946: 814,907 visitors to the park. The 1947 season opened with promise of another great year for the park.

Yellowstone National Park has been administered under the Secretary of the Interior ever since its establishment. There were civilian superintendents from May 10, 1872, to Aug. 20, 1886; army officers detailed as acting superintendents, from Aug. 20, 1886, to 1916, at which time the National Park Service of the Department of the Interior was established. From October 16, 1916, to the present time, civilian superintendents have guided the destiny of the park—the present superintendent being Edmund B. Rogers, who has served in that capacity ever since May 25, 1936.

ADMINISTRATIVE OFFICERS
PRESIDENTS AND SECRETARIES OF THE INTERIOR

The Act of Congress establishing Yellowstone National Park was signed by President Ulysses S. Grant on March 1, 1872.

The National Park Service of the Department of the Interior was established to administer national parks and monuments, on August 25, 1916, by an Act of Congress signed by President Woodrow Wilson.

Presidents of the United States	Secretaries of the Interior Name	State	Appointed
U. S. Grant	Columbus Delano	Ohio	Nov. 1, '70
U. S. Grant	Zach. Chandler	Michigan	Oct. 19, '75
R. B. Hayes	Carl Schurz	Missouri	Mar. 12, '77
Jas. A. Garfield	Sam. J. Kirkwood	Iowa	Mar. 5, '81
C. A. Arthur	Sam. J. Kirkwood	Iowa	Reappointed
C. A. Arthur	Henry M. Teller	Colorado	Apr. 6, '82
Grover Cleveland	L. Q. C. Lamar	Mississippi	Mar. 6, '85
Grover Cleveland	Wm. F. Vilas	Wisconsin	Jan. 16, '88
Benj. Harrison	John W. Noble	Missouri	Mar. 6, '89
Grover Cleveland	Hoke Smith	Georgia	Mar. 6, '93
Grover Cleveland	David R. Francis	Missouri	Sept. 1, '96
Wm. McKinley	C. N. Bliss	New York	Mar. 5, '97
Wm. McKinley	E. A. Hitchcock	Missouri	Dec. 21, '98
Theo. Roosevelt	E. A. Hitchcock	Missouri	Reappointed
Theo. Roosevelt	Jas. R. Garfield	Ohio	Jan. 15, '07
Wm. H. Taft	R. A. Ballinger	Washington	Mar. 5, '09
Wm. H. Taft	Walter L. Fisher	Illinois	Mar. 13, '11
Woodrow Wilson	Franklin K. Lane	California	Mar. 5, '13
Woodrow Wilson	John B. Payne	Illinois	Mar. 15, '20
W. G. Harding	Albert B. Fall	New Mexico	Mar. 4, '21
W. G. Harding	Hubert Work	Colorado	Mar. 5, '23
Calvin Coolidge	Hubert Work	Colorado	Reappointed
Calvin Coolidge	Roy O. West	Illinois	July 25, '28
Herbert Hoover	Ray L. Wilbur	California	Mar. 5, '29
F. D. Roosevelt	Harold L. Ickes	Illinois	Mar. 4, '33
H. S. Truman	Julius A. Krug	Wisconsin	Feb. 26, '46

DIRECTORS OF THE NATIONAL PARK SERVICE

Stephen T. Mather, Illinois ....Appointed May 16, 1917
Horace M. Albright, California ....Appointed Jan. 12, 1929
Arno B. Cammerer, Nebraska ....Appointed Aug. 10, 1933
Newton B. Drury, California.........Appointed Aug. 20, 1940

ADMINISTRATIVE OFFICERS
of
YELLOWSTONE NATIONAL PARK

CIVILIAN SUPERINTENDENTS

Nathaniel Pitt Langford ....May 10, 1872 to April 18, 1877
Philetus W. Norris ....April 18, 1877 to March 31, 1882
Patrick H. Conger ....April 1, 1882 to Sept. 9, 1884
Robert E. Carpenter ....Sept. 10, 1884 to June 30, 1885
David W. Wear ....July 1, 1885 to Aug. 20, 1886

ARMY OFFICERS DETAILED AS ACTING SUPERINTENDENTS

Capt. Moses Harris ......1st Cav., Aug. 20, 1886 to May 31, 1889
Capt. F. A. Boutelle ......1st Cav., June 1, 1889 to Feb. 15, 1891
Capt. Geo. S. Anderson ..6th Cav., Feb. 15, 1891 to June 23, 1897
Col. S. B. M. Young .....3rd Cav., June 23, 1897 to Nov. 15, 1897
Capt. James B. Erwin ..4th Cav., Nov. 15, 1897 to March 15, 1899
Capt. W. E. Wilder .....4th Cav., March 15, 1899 to June 23, 1899
Capt. Oscar J. Brown ....1st Cav., June 23, 1899 to July 24, 1900
Capt. Geo. W. Goode ......1st Cav., July 24, 1900 to May 8, 1901
Capt. John Pitcher ....1st Cav., May 8, 1901 to June 1, 1907
*Gen. S. B. M. Young (Retired)....June 1, 1907 to Nov. 28, 1908
Maj. H. C. Benson ......5th Cav., Nov. 28, 1908 to Sept. 30, 1910
Col. L. M. Brett ....1st Cav., Sept. 30, 1910 to Oct. 15, 1916

CIVILIAN SUPERINTENDENTS

Chester A. Lindsley, Asst. Supt., detailed as Acting Superin-
    tendent ....Oct. 16, 1916 to June 28, 1919
Horace M. Albright ....June 28, 1919 to Jan. 11, 1929
Roger Wolcott Toll ....Feb. 1, 1929 to Feb. 25, 1936
Edmund B. Rogers ....May 25, 1936 to

*Detailed as superintendent without compensation. Having been
    retired he was not commanding officer of the troops, as were
    the others in this group.

(Revisions by Superintendent Edmund B. Rogers. See MEMO-
    RANDUM for the Director, Oct. 23, 1946).

INDEX